What Works for Autistic Children

DR LUKE BEARDON

Also by Dr Luke Beardon

Autism in Adults
Autism in Childhood: For Parents and Carers of the Newly Diagnosed
Avoiding Anxiety in Autistic Children: A Guide for Autistic Wellbeing
Avoiding Anxiety in Autistic Adults: A Guide for Autistic Wellbeing

What Works for Autistic Children

DR LUKE BEARDON

sheldon PRESS

First published by Sheldon Press in 2022
An imprint of John Murray Press
A division of Hodder & Stoughton Ltd,
An Hachette UK company

5

This book is for information or educational purposes only and is not intended to act as a
substitute for medical advice or treatment. Any person with a condition requiring medical
attention should consult a qualified medical practitioner or suitable therapist.

A CIP catalogue record for this title is available from the British Library

Trade Paperback ISBN 9781399801683
eBook ISBN 9781399801690

Typeset by KnowledgeWorks Global Ltd.

Printed and bound in Great Britain by Clays Ltd, Elcograf S.p.A.

John Murray Press policy is to use papers that are natural, renewable and recyclable products
and made from wood grown in sustainable forests. The logging and manufacturing processes
are expected to conform to the environmental regulations of the country of origin.

John Murray Press
Carmelite House
50 Victoria Embankment
London EC4Y 0DZ

Nicholas Brealey Publishing
Hachette Book Group
Market Place, Center 53, State Street
Boston, MA 02109, USA

www.sheldonpress.co.uk

To Iain; you provided superb support as my Doctoral supervisor, and have subsequently supported me in ways too many to list here. Thank you for (at least trying) to keep me on track.

Contents

Acknowledgements

To my amazing students, who teach me so much.
To my amazing colleagues, who put up with me so much.
To my amazing family, who I love so much.

1
Introduction

'Now, then – for those of you who don't know me, my name is Luke ...' What??? 'Now then ...' – is it now, or is it then – surely there can't be a happy medium? One or the other, surely? And what do you mean, your name is Luke for those people who don't know you – what is your name for the folk who do know you? Why is it different? And now that I've got to know you, which moniker do I use?

The above is a slightly provocative (and fictitious) example, but one which demonstrates how important the detail (in this case of language) can be in terms of the potential impact it might have on a person. If one is autistic and has a well-developed sense of detail, a logical and unambiguous way of understanding language, with a high degree of linguistic competency, one might be forgiven (or, importantly, should be forgiven) for responding in such a manner to the opening sentence. Indeed, perhaps it is the person who has uttered the nonsensical sentence who should be seeking forgiveness. And yet, time after time, it is the autistic person who is deemed at fault in such circumstances, told they are in the wrong – and, in this example, declared as being 'impaired in communication'. When one strips back the example and views it through the autism lens – in other words understands it from the autistic perspective as opposed to the rather narrow view of only seeing things through a non-autistic perspective – it becomes clear that if such examples of miscommunication are rife, then it is no wonder that autistic people are so terribly and unfairly disadvantaged in life. And, of course, communication is but one of the plethora of areas that may cause such misunderstandings between the autistic population and the predominant neurotype (PNT). Added together, it becomes scary just how disadvantaged autistic people are, often daily, often long term, often to devastating effect.

My intention in writing this book is to highlight some of the areas of childhood that may add to that disadvantage, and propose alternatives to how society in its various differing factions might act, in order to redress the imbalance that currently exists. And make no mistake, there is a very real and hugely (negative) impactful imbalance for many, most, possibly all autistic children (adults too – but that's the next book). The level of discrimination against autistic children is difficult to discern – but I suspect it would horrify most people to learn just how insidiously society treats autistic children. Part of that horror stems from the fact that this is not even usually intentional; let's face it, most people are pretty much ok and don't wake up each morning wilfully trying to make autistic lives worse. But if autistic children's lives are being made worse by how society treats them and misunderstands them, then there is a duty of care to do something about it.

Terms

By the way, my name *is* Luke (now, then, and in the future, and to anyone whether they know me or not) – and when I write 'I', I am referring to myself. This seems rather obvious – but whereas I refer to myself, the ideas that stem from that place come from a much broader base than my own very simple brain. I am fortuitous in the extreme in that my life has long since been lived in an abundance of rich colour afforded to me by the hundreds (or thousands) of autistic people who have shared their lives with me in some way. Some of that has been directly, some indirectly. I read autistic accounts, be they formally published as books, or created as blogs; I watch vlogs; I have many autistic students as well as quite a variety of autistic connections outside of my 'professional' capacity. Not a day goes by that I don't have some direct connection to autism; my job is to think about autism and share those thoughts to the best of my ability. Sincerely, any useful ideas that appear in this book are highly likely to have stemmed from the autistic voices that I have in my life, as opposed to any particular wisdom of mine; conversely, if there are terrible ideas then you can absolutely plant the blame at my figurative door.

This raises an important point – where does autism knowledge come from? Obviously, I can only speak for myself, but my experience tells me that one simply cannot beat direct contact with autistic people to learn from – and the more the merrier. Of course, I am also writing a book which aims to impart autism knowledge, which perhaps appears to be contradictory – however, if I am able to use my position of delightful privilege of having had so many autistic people in and out of my life over the years, then that is what I aim to do. I will refer to this later in the book, but engaging with the autistic population – while sounding like a no-brainer – really is of fundamental importance for the best way forward; and yet, time and time again I see practice that, deliberately or otherwise, ignores the 'autistic voice' or simply doesn't appear to even seek it in the first instance. I'm not suggesting that it's always simple – there are, after all, many conflicting and sometimes divisive autistic opinions on a range of subjects – but to wilfully ignore any input is a dangerous path to take.

I have mentioned society already – which in a sense is a rather loose term; I use it to mean the collective population that impacts autistic children in a general sense. I am not targeting any person or group of people specifically. When I use 'we' I am referring to society in general.

Similarly, if I refer to a specific population – for example teachers – I am absolutely not referring to any one person. If you are a teacher, for example, and I have made a general reference to teachers, do not feel that I am necessarily referring to you! This book will highlight what I believe to be poor practice, but just because there is poor practice in evidence does not mean that you personally are culpable of engaging with it. I will also be highlighting what I believe to be good practice – and if you find yourself agreeing and thinking that you already do that, then brilliant. There absolutely is some excellent practice within society; I am not denying that for one moment. However, I also feel that poor practice vastly outweighs good practice in most sectors (if not all) and this is something that needs an urgent redress.

So much of the autism narrative 'others' autistic children – they are the ones who are identified as different from the PNT;

by definition, though, the PNT must be just as different from the autistic population. From this point on I will deliberately refer to PNT children when required; references to children will mean that those children are autistic.

I have mentioned the PNT – the predominant neurotype. This is a term I have used since 2008 when it was explained to me by an individual who wanted me to adopt it; I was impressed with his reasoning and did, indeed, adopt the term. Essentially, it refers to the numerical majority neurotype within a given population; it avoids the term 'typical' which for me is too close to 'normal' with its subsequent connotations of 'abnormal'. Within the context of the book PNT will be used to refer to the neurotype that the majority of the population would align with, whilst acknowledging that by my own definition there are situations within which the PNT is actually autistic! Just to be clear – PNT within this book *always* relates to the neurotype that is most commonly found as a majority within society as a whole. Otherwise, within, for example, an autism-specific school the PNT would be autistic. Essentially, the PNT will refer to individuals who would not be considered neurodivergent.

However, neurodiversity is clearly a reality, and there are neurodivergent populations who would not be considered PNT but would also not invariably be autistic either. All autistic individuals are, by definition, neurodivergent, but not all neurodivergent children will be autistic. There may be all sorts of overlaps between neurodiverse populations in terms of experiences, and perhaps some of the suggestions later in the book might be useful to other neurodiverse individuals. Indeed, there are many convincing arguments to suggest that plenty of practice that suits children will also benefit the PNT children; it is unendingly frustrating to hear staff within education proclaim that what is being suggested as good autism practice would suit everyone – the fairly obvious response then being, 'well – why aren't you doing it then?'

There are times when I provide 'the autistic voice' in the form of narrative; each of these examples has a pseudonym. Some of these are real examples given by permission, others are fictitious.

What the book is for

Trigger warning: this book is based on the premise that currently we are getting it (in the main) wrong. I make no excuses in identifying just how wrong we are getting it because hopefully this can subsequently identify just how necessary change actually is. However, this may also be distressing to read. Ironically enough, it might also be distressing to read sections that aim to change practice; the identification of what I believe to be good practice may be triggering, as it highlights what is not currently standard practice.

When I suggest that we are currently getting it wrong I really do mean it. I feel that almost everything autism-related, from language use through to education and beyond, needs some level of investigation and potential shake-up if our aim is to improve autistic quality of life. Make no mistake – autistic children can be perfectly content and lead happy, healthy childhoods giving them a great chance of extending that position into adulthood. And yet my experience tells me that this is the exception rather than the norm. This has to change. Which is the purpose of this book. My hope is that by identifying some of the areas of practice that could be changed for the better, we can start to make progress and subsequently have a positive impact on autistic children. Conversely, if we don't make changes, then we are in very real danger of continuing the risk of harm to autistic children that has severe consequences.

Take my opening quotation as an example; imagine that your brain has a very specific and precise way of understanding language, and on your first day of school your teacher comes out with that statement. The potential for harm is as follows from the autistic child's lived experience:

- Can I believe him?
- Trust
- Anxiety
- Loss of focus
- Teacher's perspective
- Exclusion.

First of all, my teacher has made what I can only describe as a bizarre statement about his name. He starts off with an oxymoron and continues with the indirect assertion that his name differs between populations of kids who know him and those who do not. This is confusing and not at all what I believe to be the case. I don't for one moment believe that he is called anything but Luke, irrespective of whether one knows him or not. If I am right, and I usually am, then this guy is telling us something that is untrue; how do I now decide, from this point on, whether to believe what he says?

If I can't believe everything he says, then how am I supposed to have any trust in him? Trust is important to me – being in an environment in which I don't feel safe is extremely worrying to me, and elevates my anxiety to a degree that will become untenable unless someone does something about it. As my anxiety increases, it has a direct correlative impact on my ability to focus on what the teacher is saying and what is going on around me; I am losing the ability to follow instructions and getting more and more agitated as I ruminate on his words and try desperately to work out if I can trust this person of so-called responsibility. The more anxious I get, the more overwhelmed I become, and the greater my need is to go into fight or flight mode.

At this point the teacher is making all sorts of judgements based on my behaviour. It is clear to him that I am no longer following instructions and he is repeating his directive of 'sit down' over and over again – little does he understand that my brain is now at the point of no return and try as I might there is no way I can either understand his instruction or follow it.

Lastly, my attempts at survival mode which entail me trying my very best to escape from the classroom lead to my parents being called to come and collect me from school and my reputation as a trouble-maker begins. This reputation will follow me throughout my school years. As an adult I remain scarred by the trauma of that incident which subsequently dictated how I was treated thereafter in my formative school years.

One might argue that the above is spurious hyperbole – but the reality is that while it is an imaginary scenario, many adults will have similar stories to tell. And to reiterate – this is the outcome based on a single sentence uttered by someone who had no intention whatsoever to do any harm. What can be done about this, then? Well – this is what this book is all about. Having the knowledge of the impact we have on the children we care for is a pretty good starting point. In this particular instance, imagine how different life would be if the appropriate pre-education knowledge development had taken place, so that the teacher in question had a good understanding of the communication profile of the child. He might have been able to put any number of options in place to avoid distress; for example, he might simply have invoked a rule: 'If I say anything that you find puzzling, ask me straight away to explain myself to you.' If he then admitted that to some people his words could be confusing, accepted that words are indeed an area of great interest and linguistic interpretation was important, then a healthy and trusting relationship could blossom. Again – no hyperbole – such simple changes can dramatically influence entire childhoods, and beyond.

Repetition and apology

I am well aware that within the previous four books I have authored I have written about all sorts of autism-related material; if any of what I write in this book seems either repetitive or similar in nature to what I've previously authored, I apologize. Or do I? In a sense, the reason why themes crop up again are because they are so important, in which case perhaps no apology is required. On the other hand, if you feel that in reading this you've not gleaned anything that you couldn't have gleaned from previous reads, then feel free to be annoyed, but please do accept my apology.

How the book will be written

I am positive that as soon as I complete the writing of the book there will be numerous components that I regret leaving out. Just as my students occasionally grumble that they have a word limit imposed on their assignment submissions, so I feel aggrieved that there is a word limit to this book. There is no way I can include everything that requires attention in the autism world in relation to children. What I have done, though, is identify some of what I regard to be key aspects that relate most obviously to autistic wellbeing – something that is desperately close to my heart. Far too infrequently do we refer to autistic wellbeing when, in fact, it should be at the forefront of every single aspect of life that influences the child. Literally everything that we do to support the child should have their wellbeing proactively taken into account; it should be the raison d'être of everything we do.

Throughout the book I will choose an element of practice (practice being used in a fairly loose way – meaning something that has the potential to influence, directly or indirectly, the wellbeing of the child) that I feel could do with improving. In the main I will go through a three-stage process for each component:

1   Identification of what is current practice
2   My view on why such practice might be problematic
3   What we could do to change that practice to work towards the concept of autopia.

Concept of autopia

Autopia is a neologism created to stand for 'autistic utopia', in other words an environment that is best suited to the autistic population. While More's original island of Utopia is imaginary, autopia is something that I sincerely hope will become a reality at some stage in the future. This 'What Works' book is all about working towards an autopian future in which children can thrive and live happy, healthy lives alongside their PNT counterparts.

The (autistic) child

By 'autistic child' I mean just that – nothing less, nothing more. We know that there are all sorts of things within any child that could influence the outcome for him, her, or them. Being born blind, for example, will generate a different set of issues compared to being born with sight; being of an ethnic minority, having a learning disability, having diabetes – all of these are examples of how the child might need to be supported in ways that differ from other children. It would be impossible to go through an autopia for each of the various permutations that are possible, but the one consistent factor for the suggestions I make is autism.

2

Language and concepts

What is autism?

Pretty big question to start with! In fact, this would be an area that I could start with in terms of critique. Current practice is such that – believe it or not – there *is no consistent and accepted single definition of autism*. Certainly there are sets of diagnostic criteria (more on this later) but in terms of a definition a simple internet search will come up with all sorts of differing terminology and narratives that purport to define autism. This is hugely problematic as if we can't even agree amongst ourselves in a consistent manner what our understanding of autism is, then it will logically be rather difficult to collectively make headway into doing the best we can to improve autistic quality of life. In fact, it would be remiss not to take a moment to discuss what I mean by autistic quality of life as this is also an area of potential problem.

Current practice around quality of life far too often revolves around the PNT attempting to decide what quality of life should look like for the child – when, in fact, all they are doing is making the erroneous assumption that their own indicators of quality should be the same for the child. *This is potentially very poor practice.* What might be a suitable indicator of quality of life for the PNT child may actually be an indicator of poor quality of life for another child. One of the most obvious examples that springs to mind is that of friendship. Too often we will hear statements such as 'she needs to have more friends' or similar. I feel that the sentiment is coming from a good place – the presumption being that additional friends will improve her quality of life. Indeed, for some children this may well be the case. But is this the case for all children? Just because many of the PNT enjoy having lots of friends, it is not something that should be used as an indicator of quality for *all* children. Some children will prefer to have a very limited number of friends or even no friends at all. The latter example means that a more realistic goal for those wanting to improve quality of life, rather than working out how to increase her number of friends, might be more along the lines of how best to support her in being happy on her own. This doesn't mean that by allowing her the opportunity for safe space on her own we are doing anything wrong, even though this may be frowned upon by others; the reason they are frowning is because they don't understand that she is sublimely happy being on her own, and deeply grateful to us for giving her that opportunity. In the future, when she decides to increase her friendships, she will do so. But to be forced into doing so before she is willing or ready is not doing her any favours at all.

So – current poor practice is that too often autistic quality of life is dictated by PNT measures of quality that don't take autistic need into account. Autopia practice will understand that quality of life is likely to be different for the child, and that his needs *must* be taken into account *and understood* before we can identify what will create a good quality of living. Autopia recognizes that by imposing PNT quality of life measures onto the child increases risk of problematic practice, and that individually discerned autistic quality of life measures must be sought in order to best meet the needs of the child.

Back to the lack of consistency over an autism definition. While I still have my browser open, I shall share with you the narrative of the first three that appear after having searched for 'definition of autism'. The most striking aspect of them is the dehumanizing, pathologizing and deficit-based language that is used. The term 'disorder' is frequent, as are 'condition', 'impairment' and 'difficulty'. It is no better within the images, where a missing puzzle piece in the brain is common (presumably to denote that there is something missing in an autistic brain), and language continues (in the main) along an extremely deficit-based orientation.

More 'official' sources are the diagnostic criteria that can currently be found within the *DSM-5* (2013). *DSM* stands for *Diagnostic and Statistical Manual of Mental Disorders*, published by the American Psychiatric Association. Straight away – before I've even looked in the manual – I have problems with this. Perhaps the most obvious is that autism (or, more accurately, the *DSM* refers to 'autism spectrum disorder') is within a manual produced by a psychiatric body, and the second is that the manual refers to mental disorders. I am not in the least bit convinced that autism is a psychiatric illness or a mental disorder. In fact, it is fair to say that I proactively disagree that autism is either of those and reject the notion of autism as a psychiatric illness or mental disorder completely. But my issues only start here. The main body of diagnostic criteria consists of 436 words. Within the first 145 of these, the word 'deficits' is used five times. In the criteria as a whole 'abnormal' or 'abnormalities' is used three times; other language such as 'symptoms' and 'disturbances' also litters the text. The pathologizing language is plain to see and makes for difficult reading – the very clear message is that to be autistic one must be seen as lesser, impaired, abnormal and/or disturbed. Surely it would not be beyond the realm of possibility to change the terms to make them less dehumanizing, assuming that autism remains within those texts? Even using terms such as 'different' is better than 'disordered', for example. We are currently in a vicious cycle whereby these manuals are used as a starting point to identify autism – and parents and adults are essentially being told that they fit into an impairment – based model which makes them autistic. Individuals will often believe this as it is what is written in the medical manuals, which leads to an often life-long belief that a child or self is not as good as the rest of the population. This will often lead to masking, low self-esteem, poor mental health – patterns that are far too often seen within the autistic population.

Within an autopian concept, the first thing to change would be the terms 'diagnosis' or 'diagnostic criteria'. We don't have a set of criteria for the PNT, nor do we feel the need to pathologize them with a diagnosis. I love the concept of identity, and for autistic children to be identified as such – and I think it's extremely important. However, I am far less convinced that using the word 'diagnosis', with its very medical-based, negative terminology, is right. It would be simple enough to replace 'diagnosis' with 'identification', but the 'status' of being identified to remain the same.

Autopia would also seek to hone an autism definition with the autistic community that can be used consistently, that actually reflects the autistic experience, and that fully rejects pejorative and negative language. The definition that I created in 2017 is as follows:

Autism is a neurotype that leads to:

- a cognition that is qualitatively different from that of the PNT in the way that information specific to communication, social interpretation and interaction is processed and understood
- a perceptual reality of the sensory environment that differs considerably from one individual to the next.

These lines were the ones that took by far the longest to create in this entire book – it's not an easy task to create a definition that actually aims to mean something, is applicable to all individuals, and is not overly long. Whatever the definition, the key points from an autopian perspective are that the definition has to be agreed upon by the autistic tribe and that it is used consistently amongst all professionals. Until there is autistic-led consistency, the definition of autism will continue to require work.

Identification criteria are a very different issue to that of a definition. It is perhaps uneasy to even suggest that children can be identified within a set of criteria at all – and yet autism exists, children exist, and it is usually of great benefit for the child to be identified with the autistic neurotype for reasons I will come to later. Perhaps it's a case of starting a list of common autistic thinking and processing styles to be built on. My list, while not aiming to be identification criteria, would include the following as ways of beginning to understand whether a child is of an autistic way of being (further explained on page 51):

- Differing sociality
- Interesting and unusual imagination
- Processing language (verbal and non-verbal) in different ways
- Having a spiky profile
- Sensory sensitivities – hyper and hypo
- Passionate interests
- Hyper-focus

- Ability to process huge amounts of information
- A tendency towards a cognition that prefers order and logic.

Language/terminology/attitude

Language matters. It matters to the child, the parent, the sibling, the grandparent, the teacher, society – you name it, language matters. Never underestimate the subliminal impact of absorbing language without question and the long-term effect that might have on any given individual and/or wider population. It might be one of the most frustrating aspects of working in the autism field that the language debates and terms used are so contentious – and yet it is easy to understand many sides of the argument. As someone with strong opinions, I have my own view on autism terminology, but absolutely accept that others will have rather differing perspectives. For me, any language that sets out to pathologize autism and/or is pejorative in any way is a non-starter.

Let's be clear here – Being autistic is, by definition, to be different to the PNT in some way. And yet, *everyone* is different in some way to *everyone else*. So, does this make the point about autistic people being different actually meaningful in the great scheme of things? My answer would be a resounding 'yes'. I reject those notions that centre around any of the following arguments/ assertions:

- Autism doesn't exist
- Everyone is a bit autistic
- Autism is a disorder
- Autism is a condition
- People suffer from autism
- Autism is a spectrum.

Autism doesn't exist

Well, if autistic people exist – and they do – then autism also exists. It's pretty much as simple as that. If one accepts that there is something inherently different about the way in which a child's brain processes information compared to the PNT then that difference must be aligned to something – in this case, autism. If the brains were to process information in the same way, then there would be no difference, and it would be easier to accept that autism was a misnomer. But it simply *must* be the case that autism is very _real_, and very significant. Taking a simple example, two children – one autistic (for the sake of argument) and one PNT – are sitting in a room, minding their own business, and a fire alarm goes off. The PNT child jumps up and exits the room, while the autistic child covers her ears, crawls to the corner, and huddles up there. In this example, the responses of the two children are markedly different: why? In my view, the auditory information (the fire alarm) has been processed in completely different ways. The PNT child recognizes that the alarm is a signal of danger, recollects his 'training' in relation to what to do when a fire alarm has been set off, and leaves the room. The autistic child processes the alarm as physical pain due to auditory hyposensitivity and does what she can to alleviate the pain and comfort herself. It is very easy to argue that the two brains are processing information differently. What can explain this? Could it be that the girl is autistic and the boy a PNT? Certainly, it would not be possible to provide that as irrefutable evidence of the case, but this is only one example. Given time there will be other examples that add to the evidence base. The point is, the reactions of the children as a result of processing are very different – therefore, difference *must exist*, which is the starting point of the argument that autism is very real indeed.

This is a similar argument to one of my pet hates, which is the expression 'it happened for no reason' – which is one of the most obvious examples of a blatant oxymoron I can think of. If there were no reason, it would not have happened – it's as simple as that. Similarly, there may be all sorts of reasons behind why one child may react differently from another in the same situation – and autism is one of the explanations. To take this a stage further, autism could be seen as a 'category' of a population – in the same way that the PNT are also a 'category'. Other examples are plentiful, you can take your pick, but could include the categories of height, weight, hair colour, race, sexual orientation, being pregnant, the list is pretty much endless. The point is, just because you might belong to a specific category does not make you any less individual.

By the way, you may be thinking that being autistic, based on the example above (the fire alarm), is problematic. I would refute that. In the example above, specific to that child, the problem is the fire alarm, not the child. The child cannot be 'blamed' for having auditory sensitivity – but those in the know *can* be blamed for not installing an alternative alarm to denote fire which the child could respond to in the same way as the PNT.

Autopia's best practice is a pretty simple one – total acceptance by society that autism, and therefore autistic people, exist. This might sound somewhat ridiculous – but believe me, it's not. There are still, to this day ('this day' being 2022), people who refute the existence of autism, which can be so damaging for the child and the family. For a parent to discuss their child being autistic with a professional who refuses to accept that this is a reality is a recipe for disaster (usually for the parent).

Everyone is a bit autistic

Well, no. One is either autistic or one is not. In a similar way to those categories identified above, one is either five foot five or one is not. One is pregnant or one is not. And so on. I absolutely acknowledge that people might experience certain aspects of life in similar ways – but this does not make them (automatically) part of the same category. Being neurodivergent (but not autistic) is highly likely to mean that a child will be more likely to experience life in more similar ways to an autistic peer than, for example, a PNT – but that does not make the child autistic. The same could be said of people who are socially anxious, for example. But the individual reality is that one is either autistic or not – there can't, to my mind, be any cross-over where one is of more than one neurotype – it's just not neurologically possible in my view.

The problematic aspect of the notion that 'everyone is a bit autistic' is that it totally demeans the autistic experience and glosses over the very real differences that being autistic involves.

Autism is a disorder

The negativity in relation to the word 'disorder' must not be underestimated. As noted at the start of the section, language matters. To be referred to as disordered, to have your child referred to as disordered, to be labelled as disordered – at the very least it's not very pleasant, but more than that I do not accept that it is accurate. I don't find autistic people as a whole population are disordered in the slightest. In fact, many folk are highly ordered in their thinking and processing, quite the opposite of disordered.

If the continuous narrative around autism is one of this ilk – that of negative, pejorative, punitive language – then it will have an impact. Society will come to believe that autistic people *are* disordered, which is not a far cry away from the notion that autism needs 'fixing' or, worse, 'curing'. Additionally, to preach this 'version' of autism as a negative, disordered state to parents is to increase the chances of those parents feeling that there is something wrong with their child that requires attention – as opposed to understanding autism as a qualitative neurological *difference* which requires a differing type of parenting and support compared to the PNT. The latter is much more likely to change the whole concept of autism and, therefore, one's understanding of the child.

Getting rid of the word 'disorder' and referring to autism simply as autism seems to me to be a vast improvement. Not only is it more accurate to remove the 'disorder' but it is a step towards understanding autism as a part of the human condition that is neither better nor worse than any other neurological difference. We must never lose sight of the disadvantages that face children in current society, but we *can* start to redress the balance of blame whereby the problem lies with the child, not society.

Autism is a condition

No – autism is a component of a human being (much like the categories identified above) – it is not something that is an add-on problem. 'Conditions' are often viewed as illnesses or similar that require 'treatment' – sometimes, with the suggestion that with the proper treatment there will be a resulting cure for the said condition. Autism is autism – not a condition that requires a cure.

It might seem trivial to play about with words – but it really is not. Compare the following sentences:

- The child has an autistic spectrum disorder – the child is autistic.
- My child has a condition called autism – my child is autistic.
- Your child needs treating for autism – your child might need a different parenting style.
- Autism needs to be cured – autistic children need understanding in a different way to other kids.

Changing the narrative around autism is not only likely to have a very real impact on the child's life, it doesn't even cost anything to do!

At this point I must be very clear: I do not, and never will, underestimate the problems that many children and families face as a result, in part, of autism. However, I absolutely believe that this is not because of autism per se – but because of the environment around him. The fire alarm, as an example, is one where autism might be 'blamed' – as opposed to understanding *and accepting* that being autistic is a difference, so the environment is likely to require differences to suit the child. If, hypothetically, PNT children were all super-sensitive to the noise of fire alarms and found the noise of auditory alarms acutely painful, then it would be relatively easy to see a scenario in which fire alarms were visual rather than auditory (or any other solution that avoided causing pain to PNT children); in this hypothesis, switching around the experience of the PNT child with the (autistic) child demonstrates that environments are (usually) set up to suit that majority – the PNT – and where there is a different neurotype (in the minority) it is that neurotype that becomes the 'problem'. Taking this a stage further, I genuinely believe that being in the minority (i.e. being autistic) leads to all sorts of problems as a direct result of environments *only* suiting the PNT; what is appalling, in my view, is that any issue that subsequently stems from the child for whom the environment is unsuitable is blamed on the child being autistic – as opposed to any acknowledgement that it is the environment that is the cause of the problem, not the child. This is a somewhat simplistic argument that culminates in the concept that autistic children are being targeted simply for being a minority group – which, incidentally, is exactly what I believe frequently happens.

Removing 'condition' (along with 'disorder') reduces risk of autism being seen somehow as an 'add-on' rather than a part of being human. It also reduces the risk of it being seen as something that requires treatment or cure.

People suffer from autism

Being autistic does not equate to suffering – therefore it is blatantly incorrect to assert that people suffer from autism. Many children will suffer at the hands of a society that does not understand, accept, make accommodation, adjust and respect them – that is absolutely the case, and that is equally as absolutely what needs to change. An analogy that works for me is the child who is suffering from being racially abused. Does that mean the child suffers from 'blackness'? Or is the child suffering because of the people who don't understand, accept, make accommodation, adjust, and respect them? In this instance do we attempt to somehow make the child 'less ethnic' to 'fit in'? Find a treatment? Treat the child as if he has a condition? Leave things as they are and just accept that being in an ethnic minority means that a child is more at risk of suffering? Or do we do what we can to strive to make the world a more equitable space and balance out inequality issues by changing the environment to best suit the child?

So – what to do about it? Accepting that many children absolutely do suffer, but also accepting that they don't suffer simply because they are autistic, means that we have to acknowledge that if the suffering is going to change, then we need to do something about it. If we also recognize that a child will always be autistic (which they will), then if suffering is to be alleviated it is down to other factors that *can* change in order for the suffering to change.

Autopia is based firmly in the equation that I cite at every given opportunity, that of **Autism + Environment = Outcome**. I have written and spoken about this extensively elsewhere, so while I have included my apology early for potentially being repetitive, I shall endeavour not to dwell too much on this equation at this stage – no doubt I will refer back to it at other points in the book. However, suffice to suggest here that autopia recognizes that as autism is a part of the human being that cannot be changed, the focus to alter the outcome for the autistic child should in the first instance always be the environmental factors that influence them. There are myriad environmental influences, and I aim to cover some of them throughout the book.

Autism is a spectrum

Over recent years it has become increasingly common to refer to 'the autism spectrum' (or similar). In fact, the current diagnostic label is 'autistic spectrum disorder'. The main reason for this, I believe, is to denote the individuality of humans who are autistic and to attempt to move away from the notion that all autistic people are the same. You may think this is a good thing – in fact, it is – however, the resulting notion of a 'spectrum' I feel has been made problematic by the rather two-dimensional visual that the spectrum demonstrates. If there is a linear version of a spectrum, then what do the two ends represent? In a similar vein as the earlier section on terms, this may seem, at first sight, somewhat trivial. Lurking under the seemingly innocuous concept of a spectrum, however, is a rather more dangerous beast. Or, rather, three dangerous beasts. One beast is called severity, the second function-ality, the third eccentricity. We are trained to read and process from left to right – and with the spectrum there is the temptation (at the very least) to apply some kind of 'value' in some way to this idea of a spectrum. While not invariably the case, far too often one end is seen to denote some kind of more 'severe' autism, and/or a child who is referred to as 'low-functioning', while at the other end of the spectrum terms such as 'mild' and 'high-functioning' abound. The third beast is also to be found at the right-hand end of the spectrum, whereby the notion is that just a little nudge more to the right moves a person from autistic to non-autistic in some kind of seamless fashion. *None of these notions is helpful*. Or, more precisely, none of these is helpful when referring to a child 'simply' in relation to being autistic.

I argue that there is simply no such thing as mild autism, or low-functioning autism. I absolutely do argue that the impact of being autistic in the right environment might be advantageous, or that in the wrong environment a child may require all sorts of support to function well – but these are, of course, a result of the juxtaposition of the child *and the environment* – so labelling a child as mild, severe, high- or low-functioning, without taking the environment into account appears to me to be nonsensical in the extreme. The same child will function extremely well in one environment and appallingly in another. The same child might appear to be severely affected by being autistic in one environment while thriving magnificently in another. Almost all (if not all) children will be real-life examples of these. There may be other factors to consider when it comes to functioning labels (the child with additional disability, for example). I certainly acknowledge that – but autism in and of itself should never be considered within the functioning umbrella unless the very specific child/environment combination is understood.

While the above representations of autism are flawed, we do need to have a good representation that actually identifies autistic differences while moving away from functioning labels and notions of severity. Luckily, others are way ahead of the game here and autistic people have done a superb job of coming up with terms such as 'constellation', as well as very useful graphics that are multi-dimensional (often circular) that can be an excellent alternative to the outdated concepts of a linear spectrum. Autopia bows down to those at the forefront of the visual representation brigade and I would urge you to follow the lead.

Identity-first language

You will have noted that 'autistic child' is my preference over 'child with autism'. In other words I choose identity-first over person-first language in relation to autism. Others will have their own thoughts on this, but my rationale is as follows:

- Autism is an inherent part of the child.
- Person-first language suggests an add-on.

Being autistic is for life, there is no doubt about that. My feeling is that identity-first language accepts and embraces that fact as a neutral, factual statement that doesn't in any way seem to judge. Person-first language on the other hand seems to me to suggest that autism is something that can be dealt with separately from the child as a discrete entity – much as the word 'condition' suggests. To me, this is never going to be the case, so identity-first terms are better suited to the child; there are possible wider connotations, too – owning one's self as an autistic child suggests a sense of self-satisfaction, even pride, that person-first language negates to a certain degree.

Autism as a moniker itself

Just to really throw the proverbial spanner in the works, it is useful to investigate the word 'autism' itself. Before I do this, it must be clear that the autistic tribe are very much claiming autism as their right, so this small section can safely be understood as a comment that is important to make, rather than a plea for autism as a moniker to replaced with something else.

'Autism' combines the Greek *autos* (shortened to *aut*) meaning 'self' with the equally Greek *ism* meaning 'state of being'. The connotation of this appears to be that autistic people are somehow self-orientated, inward looking, and possibly even egotistical (the latter being very much an historical theory). These connotations are extraordinarily misplaced – many children will be diametrically the opposite of self-orientated, inward-looking and/or egotistical. It may not appear that way based on a child's behaviour – but far too often that behaviour is understood only from the PNT perspective, as opposed to through the autism lens – in which case a very different understanding can emerge. Autopia recognizes that autism as a moniker is here to stay – but also suggests that the origins of the word are not to be taken at linguistic face value.

Why language is damaging

One might be forgiven for thinking that so far I have spent far too much time on aspects of autism that bear little resemblance to autistic quality of life – words are, in the end, only words. However, I feel that what we hear in terms of words is the veneer over which a far more unsettling reality is (partially) hidden. Sometimes this reality pokes its extremely ugly head through and bites viciously – ask any parent and, sadly, the chances are that they will provide ample examples of how people really view autism. I don't for one moment think that society is deliberate in its pervasive negativity, I suspect it's an historical hangover more than anything else, based on misinformation and outdated theory that still impacts current thinking. However, I feel just as strongly that the negative narrative veneer *is* an indication of autism being seen as problematic. I make mention of trigger warnings earlier on – this is perhaps a timely reminder that some of what I write about is deeply disturbing.

My premise – based almost entirely on an understanding of the language used and attitudes so often expressed – is that autism, by which I really mean autistic people, are still, to this day, seen somehow as lesser. So much of the tone associated with autism – direct and indirect – is that of autism being a problem that requires fixing. An autistic child is deemed autistic, for example, by being judged (and I use that word very deliberately) against a perceived 'norm' – with the understanding that being a disordered or impaired norm is an indication of autism. This is without a shadow of a doubt an example of autism being seen as 'lesser'. This is but one example amongst a proliferation of examples that can be seen across society. The tragedy model that supports the notion that parents of children must go through a grieving process, the headlines bemoaning an autism epidemic, the disgraceful dark side of abusive, manipulative traders of so-called 'cures' – all of the above are day-to-day norms that autistic people are exposed to; the impact on autistic wellbeing in response to these messages is incalculable.

Autopia absolutely accepts that being autistic in the current climate is to be at a major disadvantage, and acknowledges how problematic life can be for those many children and their families. However, autopia also absolutely rejects the medical model of autism that firmly situates the problem with the child; autopia promotes the concept that difference does not and should not equate automatically with disorder or impairment, and that the autistic brain is by no means inferior to that of the PNT. Autopia would consist of environments in which every aspect of language that pathologizes and creates negativity towards children is banished. Neutral or positive language will only ever be the acceptable narrative in relation to autism whilst accepting – like all populations – that children will also need higher levels of support in some areas than others in order to achieve their own quality of life goals.

In a similar vein there would be a rejection of the othering of children, and an eradication of pointing out a child being autistic in either a negative sense or in stories in which it is irrelevant. Indeed, it would be a criminal offence for the media to identify a child as autistic in a story in which it holds no relevance.

Longer-term impacts of being seen as lesser

I am a firm believer that childhood experiences go a long way towards shaping one's lived experiences throughout life; I know this isn't exactly rocket science, but, if not, why does society seem to blindly ignore what children are exposed to in the autism world without taking into account the very real and very disturbing risk of negative implications longer term? Why are children continuously exposed to an ongoing message that they are impaired, disordered, inferior and lesser? What would it cost to eliminate the use of terms that degrade children and potentially harm them for life? If you are told, directly or otherwise, that a fundamental component of who you are is something undesirable, it is no wonder that you will grow up feeling undesired. It is no wonder that you will be less likely to like yourself, suffer from low self-esteem, and strive to be someone that you will never be. Conversely, if you are accepted, loved for who you are, embraced (not necessarily literally – many children may be hug-averse!), even, dare I say it, celebrated – surely you will stand a better chance of living a life of high quality. The long-term impact of how autism is framed, conceptualized, understood, accepted – even revered at times – *will change lives dramatically*. It is almost beyond comprehension to me that we are still, in this day and age, not fighting harder to change attitudes – if as much hard work went into changing society's mind about autism as there is trying to change the autistic child then we might well be on to a winner.

Autopia never sees autism as a problem, refutes any notion of the child being in any way lesser, and promotes the idea that a diverse range of humans with a diverse range of thinking styles can be nothing but a useful and positive aspect of society and humankind.

The notion of the autistic 'tribe'/community

There is an increasing sense of community within the population, and the idea of an autistic 'tribe' is becoming more referred to. Not all children will want or need to feel part of a tribe, but nonetheless it might be something that could be promoted in order for the child to feel a sense of belonging that she may otherwise miss. To be different can be a very lonely state – to feel that one belongs, in a way that is meaningful, can be something that plays a positive part in childhood and beyond; such a potentially simple thing as a conversation about belonging to a tribe might make the difference between lonely misery and feeling rooted, accepted, and part of a wider population.

Autopia maintains that we are all a part of humankind, but that there is also value in aligning with others who may be like-minded individuals with shared perspectives who can offer that sense of belonging that might otherwise be missed.

Autistic pride

I have always been fascinated with the concept of pride – I've never quite understood how one can be proud of one's self per se, when we are all born to be a self, so it really isn't anything that we have control over – and, therefore, how can we feel prideful of it? As I've grown older and recognized that I am, possibly, being rather overly narrow in my understanding of the concept of pride, as well as having a broader understanding of why certain groups may fly a pride flag, I am more and more convinced that autistic pride will be a necessary concept until that day when children are genuinely utterly accepted for who they are. I feel that when minority groups promote that they are prideful, what they are saying to society is, we are not ashamed, there is nothing wrong with us, you are the ones who have imposed negativity on us and *you are in the wrong*.

Autopia is where autistic pride is a thing of the past. Autopia happily promotes being proud of who one is as a person, but is also a society in which autism is so indelibly accepted that the fight for equality and inclusion is no longer necessary.

Parallels with other minority groups

I do very occasionally wonder if this paradigm shift within society will ever actually happen. I reckon twice a year I wake up with doom and gloom and ask whether it's all worth it – not the fight for a better future, but whether that fight will ever really change anything. Usually by about lunchtime I've got a grip and realized that I'm being unduly pessimistic and that positive change can and does happen, and can and *will* happen within the autism world. One only needs to look at recent history and the terrific strides that have taken place in other areas of humanity to take inspiration and solace; we are still a long, long way off from genuine inclusion of all the various diverse groups of individuals who enrich our world – but let's face it, we are still a lot better off than we were even one generation ago, let alone two or three. The speed of change seems to be accelerating, the foundations of broader inclusivity have been laid, we just need to keep on with the building blocks until a perfect palace of acceptance has been built, within which we can all reside in our beds of equality.

Autism awareness versus understanding and acceptance

Just a quick one here – rhetorical question – why do we need to be aware of autistic people? Surely, as a society, we kind of know autism exists and, therefore, autistic children and adults exist – so what is the point of autism awareness? It seems to me somewhat patronizing, even othering, to keep having autism awareness days/weeks/events. Changing the narrative to autism under-standing, or autism acceptance, or both could be a far better way of promoting autistic rights.

Autopia, on the other hand, doesn't have autistic anything in place of autism awareness – as everyone already knows what they need to know about autism. And everyone has already embraced autism at just the right level that is required.

Spiky profile (and age)

Children will have a spiky profile – it's part and parcel of being autistic. Having a spiky profile is no bad thing – but it can be problematic unless the child is understood in the right way. Having a spiky profile essentially means that the child is more likely to be more extreme in various skills and abilities compared to the PNT. All children will have areas that they are better at than others – that much is obvious. But there seems to be more extreme versions of the PNT child when it comes to autistic children. When one is interested in something, one is extremely interested in it – and, subsequently, might become proficient within that area; if one, on the other hand, is absolutely disinter-ested in something then it is likely that one will be markedly less proficient at it. This all makes perfect sense – and yet we live in a society in which all children are deemed to require lots of skills all to a mediocre degree. I like to understand this in relation to breadth and depth – and often use medical professionals and the teaching profession as analogies.

Take a direct comparison between a GP and a specialist heart surgeon. They may share many skills, but in terms of knowledge it's safe to suggest that the GP has a wider knowledge in a general sense of illness (i.e. extensive breadth) without necessarily an in-depth degree of knowledge around heart surgery. The surgeon, conversely, may not have the breadth of knowledge around illness but a huge amount of specialist knowledge around the heart (depth). The GP and the heart surgeon have very different profiles of knowledge and expertise – and both are absolutely necessary within the world.

Some teachers – usually those working with younger children – will have all sorts of teaching knowledge around an array of subjects (breadth) while other teachers – say, for example, a university lecturer – might have a much more in-depth knowledge of a more limited field of study. Again, both are necessary and valued members of the teaching profession.

The very loose analogy is that PNT children tend to have brains that are more attuned to breadth, and the autistic child's brain tends to be more drawn to depth. This subsequently leads to the spiky profile. I feel that many people think that a spiky profile is related to a lack of ability in some areas with a conversely excellent ability in others. While this might be a resulting outcome, I think that the reason why a child ends up with a spiky profile is more to do with interest and motivation. The child is far more likely (compared to the PNT) to have a specialist passionate desire to engage in a narrower and smaller number of activities; this subsequently means that they have less time and inclination in other areas which leads to a lesser level of skill in those areas, which is nicely balanced out with a greater set of skills in the area of passionate interest. It's all about the balance of breadth and depth, and the combination thereof. Some children might have one extremely passionate interest at any given time to which they allocate as much time as possible – which makes perfect sense. However, they don't fit in with the majority way of doing things, and are subsequently disadvantaged. This disadvantage is abundantly clear in so many ways, not least in the way in which children are educated. Almost by definition there is a breadth of subjects that are taught in school – without a huge amount of depth. Ironically, the higher up the academic ladder one climbs, the more depth one is required to work at, while at the same time the breadth becomes narrower. The extreme end of academia in this scenario is the doctorate, which could very easily be described as an extremely in-depth study of one very specific issue – in many ways this can be very well suited to the autistic brain, but whether the individual can actually get through an education that is less suited to him in the first instance is another matter.

The spiky profile is not just related to academic achievement – the child is likely to have a spiky profile in all sorts of areas of life – their emotional understanding, social, communication – the list goes on. Again, I propose that the child is not *impaired* in certain areas – he is simply balancing things out. Imagine as a child that you have a certain amount of finite mental energy in which to develop skills around all areas of development, including social, emotional, speech, non-verbal communication and so on. Very simply, the more energy the child spends on one aspect of life, the less energy they have left for the others. If a child's brain is such that he has a super focus and propensity to learn in depth in one area, it is likely that his breadth of development will be limited. Again, this will lead to the spiky profile that we see in children and well beyond into adulthood.

Age will come into all of this as well; society currently has standards against which children are judged; this is in a whole host of areas of child development. There is an abundance of guidelines and/or expectations – what age a child should be toilet trained, what milestone should be reached and when – first words, counting to ten, learning their own name – almost everything related to child development seems to have a label attached to it with an expected due date. If one does not meet said expected date then the child is often seen as delayed in development or problematic. However, these due dates are based on PNT development, so, by definition, are highly likely not to be beneficial when one understands that the child does not have a

PNT brain. This constant judging against a set of pre-determined 'norms' sets the child up for failure, time and time again – and yet the areas in which the child might be quietly excelling, because they don't fit in with PNT expectations, get ignored in the main. I believe that age, when it comes to the autistic child, is far less relevant than it is purported to be within PNT expectation. Many children will demonstrate skills in certain areas that are more usually associated with children who are way older, and the converse is also likely to be the case.

Autopia rejects the notion that children should be compared against a set of norms; autopia understands that this kind of comparison is unhelpful, and likely to support the medical model of impairment-based understanding of autism. Autopia also suggests that age as a concept to determine levels of skill should be far less relied upon, and that children should be allowed to develop skills in ways that suit their autistic brain, rather than being encouraged or even forced to follow a PNT pattern of development.

Autism as an accepted and embraced aspect of humanity

Without over-emphasizing the point, autism *has* to be accepted within society as an important – in fact crucial – component of how humankind develops and thrives. Without autism the world would be a vastly different place than it is now – I fervently believe that, and there are numerous examples of individuals, some famous, others less so but still highly influential, who have changed the nature of society for the better, forever. *The same can of course be said for the PNT.* This latter point is an important one – it is the delightful combination of PNT and autistic neurologies that, if allowed, can work wonders. I am not at all sure that one population would do very well without the other.

This brings me very much back to language and the concepts of attitude and division. Autopia would be based on the principle that no one population is better or worse than another, just in the same way that no one person is better or worse than another. The diverse neurological ways in which populations and individuals think and process information should *all* be respected; autopia does not suggest that there is a 'them and us', nor does autopia believe that there should ever be inequalities for any neurological way of being. Autopia firmly believes that the juxtaposition of the PNT way of understanding the world with the autistic understanding of the world, with a healthy measure of mutual respect and willingness to work alongside one another with deference to each population's needs, is an extremely positive way of existing.

3

Professional practice

What is autism knowledge?

One of the single biggest problems facing children (and their families and carers) is lack of, misplaced, incorrect, even damaging understanding of autism. One needs a qualification to be a teacher; the same can be said for many other careers involving the support of and care for human beings. And yet it is rare to find roles that involve the support of and care for autistic children in which the same vocational qualifications are a statutory component of the job. This is astonishing – and not in a good way. Untold damage can be done to children, usually inadvertently, by individuals who do not have the requisite autism understanding. To reduce the risk of such damage, autopia suggests that the following issues need to be understood:

- Viewing the child through the autism lens
- How to critique autism theory/autism misconceptions
- Understanding intersectionality.

Viewing the child through the autism lens

Simply put, unless the child is understood through the autism lens then she will be in grave danger of being misunderstood. The autism lens is an incredibly useful concept – the concept being that unless consideration of a child's actions can take into account that child's autism and the way it impacts her at that particular point in time within that specific environment, the risk of misunderstanding the child and misinterpreting her way of being increases exponentially. Fully understanding each of these components – autism, the environment, that point in time – is essential if the child herself is to be understood correctly.

Most PNT adults will automatically view a child through a PNT lens – it is, after all, their own natural way of being. Being able to move away from that lens, and empathically (learned or otherwise) see a child from a rather differing perspective, is invaluable. It amazes me that professionals are 'allowed' to be exposed to children without the requisite knowledge as to the best way to prepare themselves to understand the child through the autism lens. My belief is that there is a direct correlation between lack of autism understanding and poor and/or damaging practice, irrespective of how well meaning the professional is. In order to see life through the autism lens one has to have autistic empathy. This might be at an intuitive level or it can be learned through study and experience. Irrespective of how autistic empathy comes about, it is crucial in order to best understand the autistic child. Empathy is an interesting concept, and there is more than one type of empathy – in this instance I am referring to the ability to understand why a child is engaging with the environment in any particular way as well as subsequently understanding the best way to react to the child. Some examples:

Mary is sitting quietly in her playgroup along with other children, while the playgroup leader is reading a story. All of a sudden Mary jumps up and starts to flap her hands. A member of staff, feeling that Mary is agitated, runs to Mary and hugs her, asking her to calm down. Mary struggles with the member of staff, trying to get away from her, and eventually manages to escape from the room. She is found several minutes later hiding in the toilets.

From a PNT perspective, this might be an understandable reaction from the member of staff. What the member of staff has not understood, though, is that Mary, being autistic, is likely to behave in ways that should not be reacted to in a PNT way. Consider the alternative:

Mary is sitting quietly in her playgroup along with other children, while the playgroup leader is reading a story. All of a sudden Mary jumps up and starts to flap her hands. A member of staff, remembering that Mary is autistic and having read her autism profile intently, and being attuned to Mary's way of autistic being, believes (rightly) that Mary is demonstrating acute and intense happiness; the member of staff reflects on why that might be the case and realizes that the storyline has made mention of a whale – and whales are Mary's absolutely favourite animals. The member of staff stands next to Mary smiling and 'silent clapping' to share Mary's appreciation, and Mary continues to listen to and enjoy the story.

Whilst this might sound like a simplistic and minor example, it is anything but. The first example ends up with a child being physically assaulted – Mary is tactile sensitive and being hugged, especially when in a moment of high arousal and without warning, is akin to abuse to her; she is forced to flee the situation and hide – all of which culminates in her getting a reputation for being disruptive and problematic. The reality is that Mary has essentially been punished for being herself. The second example shows how the outcome can be dramatically different. Taken as an isolated incident one might think that there is not really much of a problem; but if Mary goes through life with everyone only understanding her through a PNT lens, it is very likely to lead to trauma. If, on the other hand, everyone could understand Mary through her autistic lens, then the chances are much greater that she will lead a high-quality existence.

Some readers might be thinking it is not ok for Mary to 'behave' like this; sometimes I have heard arguments such as this kind of behaviour is disruptive for the rest of the group. I don't buy into these arguments at all, and consider them to be discriminatory. Presumably one has to draw a line somewhere when it comes to disruption – however, at present, there seems to be an almost zero-tolerance attitude to any behaviour that strays anywhere at all from what is regarded as a perceived norm, unless there are obvious reasons behind it (for example if a child has an obvious physical disability). I feel that if a child demonstrates excitement by stimming, and that she is encouraged to do so, others in the class would soon learn not only that it can easily be accepted but also that an exploration into all the interesting and diverse ways children express emotional states is a great learning opportunity. Creating an atmosphere such as the latter is to start the foundations of a generation of genuinely inclusive individuals.

Understanding the child through the autism lens is, I believe, literally the only way forward. Judging a child in a PNT way simply doesn't work – nor would it work if one was to attempt to understand a PNT through an autism lens. The two simply clash. In fact, not understanding a child through the autism lens is to massively increase risks of poor practice, trauma, abuse, poor quality of life, low self-esteem, poor mental health – and worse. It cannot be emphasized enough just how important it is. And yet, as a society, we continue to allow under-qualified personnel to engage with children with a vague sense of it being ok.

Here we come firmly up against a perennial issue – the tension between wanting to be inclusive and needing to give the child the best support in life. I am not suggesting that the two are mutually exclusive, but there is definitely a problem here. If we accept that only by understanding the child through the autism lens are we to give the child the best chance in life, then presumably anyone involved with the child needs to have the ability to do so. We also know, however, that being able to satisfactorily see the child through an autism lens is very likely a role that only a minority of people within society (in this case within that child's micro society) can fulfil. So what does that mean? That the child is only ever exposed to a very small number of specialized individuals – or that the child is exposed to people who might potentially be harmful to him?

Rather than understanding the issue in this somewhat binary way, though, perhaps it is – again – a case of *acceptance* in many cases rather than genuine understanding that will go a long way towards happy children within an inclusive society. Going back to Mary's example – does everyone within that environment need to understand Mary equally (i.e. with the same level of understanding)? Possibly not – if everyone has the same level of absolute acceptance, with a smaller number of key people having the ability to understand through Mary's autism lens, then this is the best fit for Mary and an acceptable way forward. After all, it is impossible for everyone in society to have an autistic empathy, however hard we strive for it. But it *is* possible to work towards everyone in society having an acceptance of autistic children, led by a smaller number of people who have a good understanding of how to see life through an autism lens. A blend between individuals with highly specialist autism lens abilities along with global acceptance with at least some level of understanding (in fact, there *needs* to be some level of understanding to allow for acceptance) seems like a good goal to aim for.

So – how does one achieve the ability to see the child through the autism lens? In a sense, at first port of call one could be forgiven for thinking that this is an impossible scenario; in fact, it *is* an impossible scenario. No one person will ever have the ability to understand all children in a genuinely empathic way. However, if we begin to understand that the autism lens is something that can be borrowed from time to time, and used in varying different ways, then perhaps we can start to work towards what is possible, rather than dismissing the entire concept as impossible.

It is also important to understand that there are different autism lenses that might be utilized in different situations and for different people. This relates to autism expertise; I don't believe that anyone can claim 'autism expert' status as a global title, but there is no reason not to believe that individuals can develop and subsequently claim autism expertise in specific areas of life. This is what autopia strives for, for example:

- A parent being expert in their child
- A counseller being an expert in understanding how therapy might work for children
- A diagnostician being expert in the identification pathway
- An educationalist being expert in the best way to support a child through the Education, Health and Care Plan (EHCP) process
- The autism expert dentist/GP/etc.
- An autism expert sleep specialist.

The list could go on and on – the point being that not everyone needs to be an autism expert for all children. Developing pockets of expertise and utilizing that expertise will go a long way to better supporting children; it also has the benefits of being financially sensible – having a small number of highly specialized professionals is surely more cost effective than trying to develop expertise amongst all of them?

How to critique autism theory/autism misconceptions

There is not enough room in this book to go through all the key autism theories and provide an in-depth critique of them; suffice to say that there is yet to be an autism theory that has been accepted by the autism community, academic community or professional community that explains autism in its entirety. I am not convinced that, in fact, it will ever be the case that a single autism theory will explain all autistic people. And why should it? Is there a PNT theory that explains the PNT population? The problem here, though, is that autism is 'taught' as an academic subject, in training sessions, as part of people's continuous professional development, sometimes as a requirement of a role such as mentoring. The plethora of training programmes, theories, courses and so on and the extremely wide-ranging content of these demonstrates, quite simply, that there is no consensus as to what should be taught to whom around autism. And yet the content of autism understanding must be essential if good practice is to prevail.

Autopia suggests that included in all training/courses/qualifications the following should be addressed:

- How to critique autism theory
- How to apply knowledge to any given individual
- How to use autism knowledge to change practice for the better.

How to critique autism theory

It is well known (in academic circles, at least) that there are criteria against which mainstream cognitive autism theory could (or should) be critiqued – and yet many training courses still 'teach' autism theory without the warning that each theory may not be fit for purpose for all autistic children. To keep it possibly excessively simple, I would suggest that *no* autism theory meets *any* academic criteria for *all* autistic people. If one were to add a criterion such as 'Does the theory explain the lived autistic experience?', then again I suspect that the theory would not stand up to scrutiny. The story might be different if one were to investigate autistic-led theory such as monotropism, which seems to be far more popular within autistic academics than any of the other mainstream cognitive theories. This isn't a book on autism theory, though – suffice to say, autism theory must be approached with caution; if autism theory is to be taught, then it must be taught with the caveat that it also needs strict critique in order to understand its flaws.

How to apply knowledge to any given individual

As noted, it might be that there will never be a neat theory that explains autism. This doesn't mean that we can't understand any given child in any given situation. I have devised the following as an example that autopia strongly suggests is adopted as a way to understand the child and work towards a specific autism lens. The model is based on the suggestion that children will differ in some or more of the following areas:

- Communicative style
- Sociality
- Sensory experiences
- Relationships
- Focus
- Processing abilities
- Learning skills
- Processing of emotions
- Belief systems

I suspect that the list could be added to, but as an example of how we might work towards an autism lens perspective it's a reasonable start. If we use these within a grid system, the below table of which is an example, then it could be a useful tool in recognizing where a child is coming from as well as identifying any specific areas that the child might require. The following is a very simplistic example of a child's day at school:

	Uniform	Transport	Assembly	Lessons	Breaks	Lunch
Communication						
Sociality						
Sensory						
Relationships						
Focus						
Processing						
Learning						
Emotions						
Beliefs						

If the relevant parties were to go through each 'box' to work out what impact (if any) there might be for the child, it would help work towards understanding what the child is experiencing and what (if anything) needs to be done about it. As noted, the example is extremely simplistic and is for illustrative purposes only.

Just to expand slightly on the bullet points for the purposes of clarity, below each one is broken down into further areas for consideration (the list gives examples only and is by no means exhaustive – in addition these should be tailored to each individual child and constantly updated as the child develops).

Communicative style:

- Expressive verbal ability
- Expressive non-verbal ability
- Receptive verbal ability
- Receptive non-verbal ability
- Accuracy of understanding language/processing of language

Sociality:

- What does the child see as a 'friend'?
- How much time would the child like to spend with others?

- Is there a preference for short, frequent interactions or less frequent but longer ones?
- What time during the day/night suits sociality?
- Is there a need for a mutual focus, e.g. gaming for both to enjoy social time?
- What causes social anxiety and what can be done to reduce it?

Sensory experiences:

- Visual
- Auditory
- Tactile
- Taste
- Olfactory
- Interoception
- Proprioception
- Vestibular
- Gustatory

Relationships:

- Is there a need?
- What are relationship motivators?
- What kind of person does the child prefer?
- Would a relationship with an animal be preferable to a person, or as an addition to other relationships?

Focus:

- Is there a specific style around focus?
- Is there a preference for hyper-focus?
- Are there motivating factors that need to be taken into account?
- Can the child switch attention easily or is this disruptive to cognitive processing?

Processing abilities:

- Does the child process more than the PNT?
- Are there different processing times for different senses?
- Are processing times impacted by specific aspects of the environment?

Learning skills:

- What is the learning profile of the child?
- Is there a preference for a specific communicative medium, e.g. visual teaching over verbal?
- What motivates the child to learn?

Processing of emotions:

- Are there any issues with alexithymia?
- Is there a shared understanding of emotional terminology?
- Might the child respond to situations (positive or negative) with an emotional reaction later than what one might expect for the PNT?

Belief systems:

- What is the status of the individual's trust system?
- What is the child's perception of time?
- What is the child's individual reality?
- What is meaningful and motivating for the child?

For me what this shows is how many areas a child might differ compared to the PNT. If anyone reading this is thinking that there is a lot to take in, and perhaps that it's too much – just think about it from the child's perspective. Each of the above bullet points could be seen as a very specific, very important, very impactful component of daily living – so *not* fully understanding it and subsequently not taking it into account through that child's autism lens is to increase risk of problems occurring for the child.

Autopia suggests that to ignore the concept of the autism lens and not to utilize it correctly for any given child in any given situation is to potentially cause harm to the child. It is imperative that those invested in interacting with children fully embrace the autism lens and take responsibility for doing all that they can to appreciate the child's lens, and to make accommodations as necessary to promote inclusion and decrease risk of anxiety and discrimination.

How to use autism knowledge to change practice for the better

So – once we have reached the autopian demands of having a better understanding of autism (i.e. better autism knowledge – with the ongoing belief that there is always more to learn), what can we do about it? The whole concept of this book might seem far-reaching, but without goals it is very difficult to aim anywhere. Having a set of standards in all areas of life that impacts on the child can at least enable us to work towards better practice, even if barriers mean that we might never achieve our goals. Many will cite financial concerns as barriers to success – quite possibly with every reason; however, without that goal in place in the first instance it is difficult to make a case for change.

In whatever capacity you are reading this, I would bet that there is an aspect of practice that you know could be improved. This might be something relatively small and specific to one individual (for example, persuading school that attendance on sports day is not in the best interest of your child) to something much broader with the capacity to influence whole communities (such as the NICE guidelines); within my course I promote the idea of an autism driver which I define as 'anything that you purport to have an influence on an autistic person or the autism population'. Basically, this covers pretty much anything that could influence a child or the wider autistic population and which can be critiqued and possibly made better. Some of the key autism drivers are ones I am covering in this book but I am unable due to both word count and lack of expertise to be able to cover as many as are applicable to all children! There are limitless examples of what an autism driver might be – which means that there are limitless opportunities for us to improve practice. From language to identification pathways to pandemic guidelines to inclusion policies and beyond, life is rich with autism drivers just waiting for you to identify and improve upon.

Understanding intersectionality

Without wishing to labour the point, the child *must* be understood both from an individual perspective and through their autism lens. But her needs will not stop there. There is an increasing awareness of the additional difficulties a child might face when there are added intersectional issues; ignoring those issues might disadvantage a child (and a family) unless due care is given. If there are presuppositions based on aspects of the child's life before autism is even considered, then autism itself may not even be taken into account. The most obvious examples that I know of in this instance include the autistic Black male who was refused an assessment for many years as those who managed such things made the (obviously erroneous) assumptions that the way in which he was engaging with the world was 'typical of a Black boy' (this was the very clear message implied to his mum) and therefore could not be linked with autism. The second, obvious example is the sheer number of women from whom an identification is kept hidden. My third example would be those with a prior diagnosis (which often turns out to be incorrect) of some kind of personality disorder. I am sure that there are all sorts of intersectionality issues for a variety of individuals; needless to say, the concept of treating all children very much as individuals needs to be at the forefront in these situations.

4

Identification

Pre-identification (diagnosis) – children

From the outset I think it's worth being absolutely clear that any child has the right to an identification; no professional at any stage should try to deter a parent from seeking an identification unless there is a very clear risk of harm to the child. It is difficult to envisage many scenarios in which this might be the case. There will be some isolated situations whereby a route towards identification might be considered inappropriate, but in the main it is the right of the family to understand if their child could be correctly identified as autistic. The vast majority of families seek an identification either to corroborate what they already believe, or to better understand their child and what support the child might require. Getting that identification could be extremely important for a number of reasons, including:

- To be believed by other professionals
- To be believed by other family members
- To access certain pathways for support
- To provide the child with their own journey of discovery.

To be believed by professionals

Being believed is something that many of us take for granted; however, for some reason – and for the life of me I am not at all sure why this is the case – many parents are just not believed. This can be within the identification process just as much as any other area of the child's life. I'll refer back to believing parents in a moment when it comes to the identification process, but in this context having an 'official' identification can be extremely useful to present to professionals who otherwise may not believe that the child is indeed autistic. It is astonishing the number of people reported by parents (and the range of professionals in those reports) who simply won't take the parents' word for granted, and either question them or even declare that they don't believe them. Having a report that categorically gives an identification can alleviate some of the incredible level of distrust which usually causes extreme levels of stress for the family.

There is also an argument that we should be seeking alternatives to the medical model-based identification, in that many parents might feel that they know enough about their child, and enough about autism, to know that their child is autistic. If this is the case, the reasoning could be that they are in the best place to make that decision, and society as a whole should subsequently respect that decision. It's an interesting and important debate, and much of the discourse around it will depend on one's framing of autism. If one believes that autism is part of the neurodiverse range of human cognition and nothing to be feared, one might think that between them the family can decide for themselves. If, on the other hand, you feel that autism is a 'condition' that needs treatment and/or intervention (as opposed to understanding and support) then you may side with the medical diagnostic process.

There are plenty of other aspects of life whereby a self-declaration is perfectly well accepted without the need for a clinical diagnosis. If someone declares themselves to be sexually orientated in a specific way, no one in their right mind would ask for some level of diagnostic proof. Similarly, if you told a school that your child was Muslim, the school would not require documented evidence. The latter is an especially good example, because within education there may need to be some adjustments made to accommodate the child – but no one would bat an eyelid at making those adjustments even though no proof of the declaration has been given. Some would argue that if families (please note, I am very deliberately referring to the *family* here – whenever possible the child should be at the forefront of these decisions) fully believe that a child is autistic then that should be enough 'proof' and subsequent adjustments should lawfully be made. Some argue that if society accepts self-identification or parental-led identification then 'everyone would do it' – but I simply don't see why this would be the case. If a child does need educating differently then she needs educating differently, whatever the reason behind it. I don't think that there is a plethora of parents waiting in the shadows to leap out and insist that their child needs all sorts of educational adjustments when the reality is that the child doesn't need anything of the sort. And if a child does need reasonable adjustments (for whatever reason), why are we not doing everything we can to provide them, without having to wait for an official diagnostic report before action is taken?

However, the current status is that families do (often desperately) need an official identification to 'prove' to society that their child is autistic.

To be believed by other family members

I believe that many people choose not to believe that a child is autistic from a very genuine place. They have a specific idea as to what autism is and the child does not fit this understanding. The flaw here, in almost every case I've ever encountered, is that the person in question has an entirely incorrect understanding of autism – in which case it is easy to understand why they can't believe the child is autistic. If we take the archaic perspective, for example (and this is to use a rather extreme example of poor understanding), that autism is a male-only state of being, then it is entirely possible – or even probable – that one will never accept that a family member's daughter is autistic. Of course, this particular misunderstanding of autism is historical (I hope), but the principle remains the same – if there is a belief of what autism is, and the belief is incorrect, then matching that belief to most autistic children will fail – which often results in parents not being believed.

In a very similar vein, if others have an extremely negative understanding of autism (which in a sense comes under the umbrella of an incorrect understanding of autism), then, again, many will refuse to believe that the child they hold dear could possibly be autistic. After all, if one sees autism as a dangerous disorder that causes innumerable problems, then how could you possibly align that model with your beloved grandchild?

Some will have autism beliefs that they have gleaned from the media, not least alarmist news reports, or from websites promoting a cure (or a cure camouflaged and wrapped in pretty pictures to draw unsuspecting parents in), or simply because they have met an identified child in the past who doesn't appear anything like the child in their family. Just a note on the latter – it is extremely odd that the word autism promotes such a miscon-strued set of responses, but one of the oddest of all is the concept that somehow all autistic children are the same. Now, we know this isn't the case, and you would be hard put to find anyone who would even hint at saying such nonsense – and yet, really, how far off is this nonsense from the proclamation that 'your child can't be autistic, she's nothing like the autistic child we met last year'. This might be forgiven when coming from a family member whose exposure to autism is limited – but when it comes from a professional who should know better it is beyond exasperating!

If in autopia there is a better, more rounded understanding of autism, then it is far more likely that parents will subsequently be believed.

To access certain pathways for support

It seems absolutely unfair that if a child has a support need relating to being autistic they can't access it unless they have a medical-based identification. The child has the need irrespective of the identification! They don't suddenly develop the need the day they get the diagnostic report through the post. And yet even today there are support systems that cannot be accessed unless the child has some level of official autism status. Some argue that this is because if those services were provided to everyone (by which I would presume the inference being everyone who needs them) then the service would be overwhelmed. The logical solution is obviously to make sure that there are enough services to meet need; to deny support based on a lack of an identification is clearly not an appropriate solution to the problem. Just a quick one on this note – I have heard far too many people far too many times argue that providing support to all autistic children whether they are identified or not is simply not cost-effective, or too expensive. This argument simply does not stand up to scrutiny for the following reasons:

- A child doesn't stop needing support just because it is denied to them.
- Lack of support very often leads to a greater need for higher levels of support later on in life.
- Support at a younger age, for a shorter period of time, may well decrease the need for additional support later in life for a longer period of time.

The first point is pretty self-explanatory. Denying support as a result of lacking an identification is simply nonsensical. The latter two points are important ones in relation to finance – and that is before the far more important acknowledgement of cost to the child and family in terms of quality of life. Financially, there is a very good argument that if support is not forthcoming then there is a greater risk of support being needed at a much more intense level as an adult. For example, almost all the adults I know who struggle with major issues, such as the law, report that had they been supported to better understand legal issues as a child, they would not have ended up in real difficulty as an adult. Lastly, what is essentially low-level support as a child might eliminate the need for support at all for the rest of the child's life – in other words, appropriate support as a child will likely decrease overall financial cost in a lifetime.

To provide the child with their own journey of discovery

Last but by no means least, providing an identification to a child may well be the first day of self-discovery for the rest of their life – in a good way. I am a firm believer that knowledge is power in a general sense – but that knowledge of self is not so much powerful as essential to wellbeing. The better one knows and understands one's self, the greater the chance of a good quality of life. Therefore, if a child is autistic, she needs to know not just that she has that identification but exactly (or as near to exactly as possible) what that actually means to her on any given day. It cannot be underestimated what the impact of fully under-standing autism, and the relationship between being autistic and one's lived experience, can be.

What to consider

This section is for those who are seeking the identification, usually parents (but not exclusively) so 'you' in this section refers to those in the position of seeking the identification.

First of all, you need to warn yourself. Giving yourself warnings can work effectively along the process, as you are already expecting problems; if those problems don't occur then all well and good; as and when they do, you have already warned yourself against them. It might even be that your warnings have pre-empted an issue and provided a potential solution. So, you might want to consider possible solutions to the following:

- *There isn't much point in getting a diagnosis as it won't change anything.*
- *I don't see any autism in your child.*
- *Your child can't be autistic because ...*

Possible answers that you could prepare before such issues arise (and feel free to use these!):

There isn't much point in getting a diagnosis as it won't change anything.

> We agree that, in a sense, it may not change anything from your perspective as a professional. However, we also feel that as a basic human right it is in our best interests to ensure that our child has the best possible understanding of their self, along with how to ensure others also have the best understanding of them. As autism is part of being a human being they will be autistic for life, so this is something that might be absolutely critical for them as an adult, even if you feel it might not make a big difference right now. We also understand that in order to prevent potential discrimination under the Equality Act it is advisable to seek an autism clarification so that our child is protected by discrimination law throughout their life. Many autistic adults report that they wish that they had been identified as a child as it may have quite dramatically changed their life trajectories in a positive way, so we feel that listening to those adults, along with the other reasons we've given, is more than justification enough to seek an autism identification.

I don't see any autism in your child.

In a sense, neither do we! However, as is often stated in autism literature and in major autism-related websites, along with multiple autobiographical accounts, masking is a very real issue and many autistic children are superb at masking while a very different scenario is being played out internally. In addition to this, autism is neurological rather than behavioural, so in many ways it would be impossible to 'see' autism anyway.

Your child can't be autistic because ...

As far as autism professionals are aware, there is nothing much that an autistic person cannot do, aside from not be autistic. It might be that certain things are far more difficult, or take a huge amount of energy, or take a very different type of energy compared to the PNT – but that doesn't mean that certain things are definitively beyond the scope of any given autistic child. Therefore, it might be less common, for example, for an autistic child to maintain eye contact (to use a rather stereotypical example) but it cannot at the same time preclude the child being autistic.

In terms of 'evidence', feel free to collate as much as possible around your child's development. In this day and age it might be that you have plenty of video footage that could be useful. It is likely that the professionals you speak to will model their assessment based on either the *DSM* (already mentioned) or the criteria set out in the *International Classification of Diseases (ICD)* – no, autism is not a disease but honestly, this is where autism criteria can be found. Do your homework and try to find out if those doing the assessment are using either of those sets of criteria, as it may help you in determining the most useful evidence base possible. They are largely similar, but there are some slight disparities between the two. It might be that you find a pathway that doesn't use either, in which case it is definitely useful to find out just how they go about ascertaining whether a child is autistic or not.

You will find – as already noted – that the current diagnostic criteria are extremely negative. They are all about locating the problem with your child and highlighting supposed impairments or deficits. This is something that you don't need to accept per se, but you will have to arm yourself against the exposure to this negative attitude towards your child – forewarned is forearmed! It might even be that as you go through the assessment process the questions that are asked are about what your child finds difficult, rather than appraising your child's overall skill set. This tends to be because the assessor is trying to match their understanding of your child against the diagnostic criteria; it might be a painful process for you to go through simply because of the model of autism that is currently central to the main diagnostic criteria. It might also be that you have an assessor who is trained in a very specific way of autism identifying, such as the Autism Diagnostic Observation Schedule. It could be very useful for you to familiarize yourself with the various ways in which people can be trained to diagnose as it may sway your decision if there are any choices that you could make (you won't usually have much of a choice to be fair, but we can live in hope).

You might find that there is a need for information to come from differing sources, so if it is possible to collate reports outside of home (the most obvious example being school) then it would do no harm to do so. Going back to my list earlier, you may decide to focus on the following:

- Differing sociality
- Interesting and unusual imagination
- Processing language (verbal and non-verbal) in different ways
- Having a spiky profile
- Sensory sensitivities – hyper and hypo
- Passionate interests
- Hyper-focus
- Ability to process huge amounts of information
- A tendency towards a cognition that prefers order and logic.

Differing sociality

See page 70

Interesting and unusual imagination

It used to be noted that autistic children 'lacked imagination'. I am not entirely sure where this came from, but it is blatantly untrue. However, much comes down first to one's understanding of what 'imagination' means anyway, and subsequently whether the type of imagination identified in the PNT, rather than 'missing' in children, is simply a differing type. I would definitely opt for the latter. In terms of definitions, it's so useful to actually define what we mean by imagination – otherwise, trying to work out if a child has a differing one to anyone else makes very little sense – in the same way, dare I suggest, that when the idea of autistic children 'lacking imagination' came about it was actually rather meaningless. Many people will identify stages of imagination in relation to behaviour, for example:

- Exploratory play
- Relational play
- Imaginary play.

Each of these stages can be defined and broken down further. The idea being that if there are developmental differences then there may be an indication of autism. It tended to be the imaginary play that got picked up on in terms of being autistic – the idea that (autistic) children lack imaginative play used to be prolific. I would argue, though, that your child *does* play in an imaginative way – but the PNT doesn't find it easy to empathize intuitively with what that imaginative play 'looks' like, so assumes (incorrectly) that it 'doesn't count'.

Some children are able to play in the imaginative PNT way, such as pretend play, but simply choose not to as to them it is a meaningless activity. This is not the same as being unable to engage. Motivation is important to all children, and unless play is motivating it is highly unlikely to entertain. Similarly, playing with other (PNT) kids might not be an option your child chooses – and why would they? If PNT children process information in a very different way to your child, and yet in a similar way to one another, it might be very difficult to feel at home in that environment. Again, it's not that your child *can't* play with other children, it's just too much of an effort.

Solitary play is sometimes deemed unimaginative – seemingly doing the same thing over and over on one's own, for example, might be termed 'repetitive play' and 'without imagination'. I don't agree. What about the child for whom watching the same video 99 times in a row allows him to 'see' something new every time? What about the child who has the ability to process all her sensory inputs at a conscious level, so *needs* to engage in a similar activity over and over again to get a different experience each time? The list could go on. When identifying your child's imagination, open yourself up to the possibility – or probability – that there is a huge amount going on within your child's brain that differs from the PNT – but is in no way 'less'.

Processing language (verbal and non-verbal) in different ways

Your child's language development is likely to be different from that of the PNT and it's worth noting what those differences might be. This includes expressive language and receptive language, both verbal and non-verbal. I genuinely feel that we have missed a trick when it comes to autistic language development, in that – as per usual – we insist on comparing it to a PNT traditional pattern of development and brand the child as 'lesser' should they not follow a similar pattern. I think it's far more useful to view the autistic population as essentially having their own language *styles* that differ from the PNT. So, for example, the same words might be used – but in a different style. Going right back to the start of the book will give examples of what I mean by this. Similarly, not using language (what could be termed as pre-verbal) is not the same as being non-communicative. It sounds so simplistic, but communication *is* a two-way process – just because a child communicates, for example, through body language rather than speech doesn't mean that they are impaired in communication – usually it means that the other person is impaired in their comprehension.

Much of verbal communication will link to the sensory processing style of your child. Some simple examples include:

- The environment
- A person's voice
- Specific words.

So – many children will be able to process voices so long as the sensory environment suits them. Being in a busy, noisy, crowded, bright, smelly classroom, for example, might make it impossible for a child to process a teacher's voice. This doesn't mean that the child doesn't understand language – it simply means that it's impossible for him to actually hear and process what is being said. The person's voice itself might be a factor that needs to be taken into account; I know some people who simply cannot abide certain pitches or tones of voice. In a similar vein, your child might delight in some words and detest others – this is often a sensory thing, though not exclusively so.

Just on that point, it is essential to remember that children may well associate language with experience, and that pain is very much a trigger for many children. So, if a child associates a specific word with a particular trauma, then subsequently hearing that word might then cause pain. I know many adults for whom phrases such as 'calm down' have an immediate triggering effect, as they associate those words with being in a high state of distress as a child, and hearing them brings back those feelings of distress.

Your child might be very precise in their understanding of language, their use of language, and their response to it. As it is such a common theme in the autism world, this has often been seen as some kind of problem – 'literal interpretation of language' being seen somehow as a problem with the child, as opposed to a problem with the language used. Being 'too pedantic' is another phrase that I often hear; I find myself wondering why such a sublime understanding of language is regarded as problematic. Breaking down examples, it is so often the case that the cause of the 'misunderstanding' is as a direct result of the verbal communication being uttered being ambiguous, ill-informed, linguistically incorrect or, simply, wrong. And yet far too often it is the child – who has processed the language accurately – who is named as the one with the problem. This is why I feel that it's worth considering language styles; neither the PNT nor the child is in 'the wrong' but a clash of language styles will increase the risk of misunderstanding – with no blame to be apportioned to either party.

Having a spiky profile

See Chapter 2.

Sensory sensitivities – hyper and hypo

See Chapter 5.

Passionate interests

Please note that the term is passionate interest – as opposed to 'obsession' or 'obsessive interests', which have rather negative connotations. The reality is that having a passionate interest can be utterly joyful; to turn this into something that seems to be looked down on in the way that 'obsessions' often are is, in my view, a deep injustice. There may be a sole passionate interest in your child's life that lasts, a sole passionate interest at any one time but that changes over time, or passionate interests that overlap. The reality for your child is that the level of interest is likely to be intense – while that brings its own potential issues, never underestimate just how beneficial a passionate interest can be.

Hyper-focus

Often in line with a passionate interest (though not exclusively by any means) your child may have the ability to focus intensely on one area of processing; this might be a sensory aspect of life (e.g. hyper-focus on listening to a tune) or it might be an activity, a person, a place – the list could go on. This again is sometimes seen as a negative – the 'accusation' being that so much focus on one thing usually leads to a lack of focus on another. To me, it's simply a preferred style rather than anything negative, and ties in very much with the concept of a spiky profile.

Ability to process huge amounts of information

Your child may have extraordinary processing abilities in that she will process all of the information around her within her conscious mind. This is vastly different from the PNT who tends not to consciously process the majority of environmental information. Ironically, this might have the impact of giving the illusion that your child has *slow* processing abilities which may not be the case at all. Being able to process 99 components within an environment takes considerably longer than processing just 9. The outcome, however, might be that processing that same 9 as the PNT will take longer, simply because of all of the other aspects that also need to be processed. Her processing speed for each individual aspect of the environment may actually be way *quicker* than the PNT – but to an observer this might not appear to be the case.

A tendency towards a cognition that prefers order and logic

Many autistic minds – though not all – lean towards order and logic to process information. This doesn't mean that your child (adults included) can't very much enjoy life that falls outside of these remits, but if you have a child who demonstrates this kind of cognitive style it is worth noting it. Having a brain that enjoys accuracy, order, rationality can be amazing – but it might also come with its own problems, especially when in company with others for whom such characteristics are lacking! So many children suffer at the hands of adults who think in less systematic ways – and yet still insist that they are in the right.

It might be incredibly useful to explore cognitive styles with your child; understanding at an intellectual level that people think differently might go some way to alleviating potential issues a child might have when facing those frustrating situations when the child feels tremendously passionately that they are 'right' in what they believe (and, in fact, usually are right) and yet those around them feel differently.

Best pre-identification processes

An autopian pre-assessment process would include the following:

- High-quality information on how to conclude whether an autism identification is something you wish to consider right now
- Non-pejorative language from the outset
- Use of autism identification as opposed to diagnosis
- Questioning as to what you are aiming to get out of the process

- Links with peers who have already been through the process
- Links with autistic adults who are able to provide expert-by-experience advice
- Contact with a key professional who would subsequently be your point of contact throughout the process, developing your unique pathway to identification together
- Absolute clarity in terms of what can be expected throughout the process, including time frames
- Absolute clarity in terms of what to expect after the process (post-identification support).

It could be extremely useful to engage with a system that has expertise and experience in supporting parents through the identification process, and to explore whether now is the right time to move forward with an autism identification. It is most likely that once you've decided that it is a pathway you wish to take then it will also be the right time! However, while I am a huge fan of early identification it must also be recognized that everyone involved needs to be in the right state of mind moving forward.

High-quality information on how to conclude whether an autism identification is something you wish to consider right now

It might be that you are extremely confident in your reasoning behind seeking an identification - some parents are aware from a very early age that their child seems somewhat different to others of a similar age, particularly if it is not their first child. However, there are plenty of parents who might need some advice as to whether seeking an identification *at this stage in their child's development is* the right option. Sometimes it's not even a case of ascertaining whether it's the right choice per se, but whether it's the right choice within the circumstances you find yourselves. Issues such as waiting lists, feedback from other parents, who might have been through the local process, whether you have the support of school and/or other family members might all need to be taken into account. Having advice from an assessment centre that allows you to make a considered, well-informed decision is something that could benefit parents hugely.

Non-pejorative language from the outset

It should be working practice to avoid any negative terminology in relation to your child; this should be reflected in any communication in any format, including literature, websites, leaflets, verbal narrative – simply, there should be a culture of zero tolerance of any negative language in relation to the child. For all staff involved, from the first point of contact through to the last, it should be absolutely ingrained that referring to autism in neutral or positive language is a natural way of being.

Use of autism identification as opposed to diagnosis

Similar to the above, changing the term from diagnosis to identification sends a qualitatively different message to parents that could make all the difference between seeking an affirmative identification compared to being put off from engaging with the process from the outset.

Questioning as to what you are aiming to get out of the process

You and your child should be the absolute focus of the whole process, and your needs must come first. Communicating with an experienced practitioner around what has got you to this point and subsequently what your expectations are for the process could help both you and the identification professionals understand what your key needs are and to aim to meet them as effectively as possible. If there are expectations that are unrealistic for whatever the reason these should become apparent at this stage and subsequent decisions made as to whether or not to go ahead.

Links with peers who have already been through the process

This should be an option provided, rather than a mandatory part of the identification. However, it might be really useful to have access to individuals and families who have already been through the process to glean real-life experiences that will enable you to have a better understanding as to what to expect, ask questions, and possibly pick up some tips as to what works and what doesn't.

Links with autistic adults who are able to provide expert-by-experience advice

Similarly, having access to autistic adults who are experts by experience could give you additional quality information as to the impact of getting an identification, how it might be communicated to your child, as well as further tips around the whole process.

Contact with a key professional who would subsequently be your point of contact throughout the process, developing your unique pathway to identification together

Many parents find themselves frustrated at the sheer number of professionals who may be involved in the process, not least because it often means that they have to repeat the same information numerous times to different people. It may well be that there are several professionals who have to be involved, but having one key contact who you can turn to at any given time and who is responsible for information sharing to colleagues could and should make the whole process streamlined and less stressful than it might otherwise be.

It is this person who is responsible for engaging with you from the start to establish how it would be best for you as a family to interact with the identification process in the least stressful manner possible. Developing your unique pathway to identification with you is essential. You can agree on aspects such as:

- What is the best way to communicate with you?
- Should there be different choices of communication at different times of the day (for example, it might be that a phone call in the evening is fine, but a text message is a much better option during the day – or vice versa!)?
- Who is the best person to communicate directly with, or should there be a group messaging service so that, for example, parents and grandparents are communicated with simultaneously?
- Where is best for you to chat with the identification team – for example, is chatting at home a preferred option or would it be less stressful to be in a more neutral environment?

- How is it best for you to share your time – would longer sessions suit, or would it be better to have more frequent but shorter sessions to glean the same level of information?
- How could you best share information – would you prefer to be sent questions via email that you can think about and respond to, or would you prefer face-to-face discussion?
- If you have an issue with any of the processes and/or personnel, what rights do you have and how would you go about making your feelings known?
- What (if anything) is anxiety-inducing about the pathway, and what (if anything) can be done to reduce anxiety as much as possible?
- If there need to be pragmatic arrangements, such as engaging with school to allow for a discussion with a key worker, who is best to make those arrangements?
- What do you feel are your child's sensory needs and how might these be taken into account?
- If anyone else involved apart from the child is autistic, or believes themselves to be, what requirements would they need to reduce anxiety and eliminate discrimination?
- Are there any triggers that need to be avoided both for the child and for anyone else involved?
- If anyone is anxious at any stage of the process how will they (or anyone else) communicate this and what is required as a result of that communication?
- What format should the final report should be in – for example, would you prefer an audio version instead of only a written one?

Absolute clarity in terms of what can be expected throughout the process, including time frames

This will be part of the role of the key worker identified above; they will work with you to prepare a time line of events including proposed time frames to establish what will be done, when, and who the key people involved are. Everyone will need to agree to this prior to the identification pathway beginning.

Absolute clarity in terms of what to expect after the process (post-identification support)

Similarly, there needs to be a clear offer as to what to expect after the pathway to identification has been completed. This should include:

- Further offers to engage with peers who have been through the process
- Information as to what support there might be locally and nationally that is 'approved' by parents and autistic adults and autistic parents
- Information as to what options you have if the result is not what you expected
- Information as to how you can seek additional pathways should the have arise (e.g. to ascertain whether an assessment for dyslexia might be useful).

What to read

I don't think it would be hyperbole to suggest that what information you engage with post-identification (or, in fact, pre-identification) is absolutely essential in terms of it being the best fit. It might be that you are in a somewhat vulnerable state, and the messages that you glean from information could make quite a difference to your attitude around yourself and your child. The internet is a tempting 'go to' but there are as many scary sites for autism information (or mis-information) as there are more positive ones; social media can be a maze to navigate, often with very differing, conflicting positions. The identification pathway should include signposts to information with a summary of what the information entails, who authored it, what background the information has come from, and whether there are levels of endorsement from previous parents and autistic adults. Free speech is extremely important, but having some level of advice as to what might be useful to read around which areas of autism experience is bound to be helpful to many parents of newly identified children.

Who to discuss with

Now that you have an affirmative identification for your child (or children) there are decisions to be made around who to disclose it to. I have written about this elsewhere, but to reiterate – one of the most important things to remember is that it is unwise to make these decisions in haste, and that once you have imparted that information you cannot take it back. I am by no means trying to dissuade anyone from sharing useful information around an identification, but you need to be in a position of awareness prior to doing so. Some questions that might be useful to consider include:

- Why are we telling this person?
- What do we hope to gain out of it?
- Will there likely be a positive impact on our child?
- Can this person be trusted?
- Will the disclosure potentially lead to problems or solutions?

The identification process – children

I am not a clinician and never have been; this section is aimed at those who are involved in the identification process in whatever capacity. I am not here to tell you how to do your job, nor am I qualified to do so. However, I do have the stories of hundreds of individuals and families to draw on, so these recommendations firmly stem from those experiences, as opposed to a critique of clinical practice. I have, however, also consulted with various clinicians involved specifically in autism identification to ensure that there is an appropriate balance.

Qualities reported to be beneficial

Parents report to me that the qualities that they have felt most helpful when going through the process include:

- Patience
- Sense of humour
- Confident knowledge of autism

- Absolute acceptance that the child in question must not be judged in any way against any other child they have assessed in the past
- Absolute belief in the parental narrative (unless there is cause for concern)
- Ability to absorb information without any judgement – anything goes
- Recognition that there may be autism in other family members
- Careful use of language
- Neutrality and/or positivity – while retaining levels of honesty
- Empathy, humility, and willingness to learn
- Making sure that the child is always the focus
- Having the ability to engage with the child as much as possible so long as it doesn't increase anxiety.

Autopian standards

The following expands on the above list of professional qualities that autopia would promote. They are in no particular order – and I wish to reiterate, I am not for one moment being critical of current clinical practice as I am not (clinically) qualified to do so; these autopian suggestions stem from the abundance of parental experiences – positive and negative – shared with me over the last few decades.

Patience

Time can be a limited commodity for parents, so setting aside appropriate time for appointments can be critical for how the parent feels they are to be treated. Hurrying a session along or cutting it short sends a message that you have other – possibly more important – things to do. From a parental perspective these sessions and time spent with you could be the most important moments in their lives as parents, so having the patience to acknowledge that and make sure you can accommodate them is important. This might be a rare opportunity for a parent to discuss their child with a professional who actually takes the time to understand and listen, so for them it might be extraordinarily precious.

Sense of humour

In some ways it might sound strange, but many parents suggest that a good balance between recognizing the gravity of the situation but without losing a sense of humour can be uplifting and make the process less stressful than it might otherwise be. No one would suggest that the child should be a centre of a joke; however, being able to see the funny side of some of the situations that families can find themselves in may assist in the relationship between professional and family.

Confident knowledge of autism

One of the most important qualities of all that I have become aware of over the years is whether the parents have confidence that the professionals involved in an identification pathway are the best placed to understand their child. It might be that the parent is extremely knowledgeable already, in which case they need to be reassured that your knowledge is at the same level as theirs (or better); or they may feel very insecure in their understanding of their child so need to feel absolutely safe in your professional hands.

Absolute acceptance that the child in question must not be judged in any way against any other child they have assessed in the past

This is in a similar vein to the previous narrative in this book – and yet it is so crucial it is worth reiterating. Parents do not want a professional to 'only' see their child as one of many; they want to feel that you are understanding that child from his or her own position without any preconceptions or comparisons with other children you will have met. Of course, the more children you have engaged with the better in a sense – that is not in question. Having extensive experience is important – but just as important is recognizing that however much experience you have, the child sat (possibly figuratively) in front of you is unique in their own right. This doesn't mean that you can't allude to potential similarities with your past experiences, more it's a case of acknowledging that while this might be the 999th child you have met, you may be the first professional that the parent has met.

Absolute belief in the parental narrative (unless there is cause for concern)

As noted earlier, parents are often not believed. Having an ethos of partnership as well as recognizing parents as experts by experience (though they may not know it themselves) from the outset is a good starting point. Not all parents *will*, necessarily, be experts in autism – but they are in a far better position to discuss their child with you than, presumably, pretty much anyone else.

Ability to absorb information without any judgement – anything goes

Some parents may be unwilling to share information if they feel that they will subsequently be judged as parents, or their child might even be judged in some way. Whenever possible, create a relationship in which parents are able to express their narrative without fear of being judged. For parents, being in an environment in which they can chat about their child without eyebrows being raised, or responses being of shock, or feeling that they will be assessed as parents can be a rare and wonderful state – and one which should be encouraged.

Recognition that there may be autism in other family members

It may well be the case that other family members are autistic themselves – some may know this, others will not. Not making any conscious or subconscious decisions over this can be so important – making the assumption that there will be a greater chance of multiple people involved in the pathway also being autistic is not a bad assumption to make. This may change the way in which you communicate and process information yourself, as well as making the process easier to cope with for the family members.

Careful use of language

I feel that as an ongoing theme, the importance of language is coming through strongly – in your case, it might be that for some families this is the first time they have actively engaged with a professional, so it's timely to note that the language that you use can shape the way in which they subsequently frame their child. Having mission statements, for example, or introductory paragraphs of text can make a huge difference to attitudes and understanding. For example, autopia pathways might have the following as statements frequently included in correspondence:

> While current terms around autism are often based on a medical, deficit-based model, and the term used to actually diagnose is 'Autism Spectrum Disorder', we reject such notions of negativity in relation to your child whilst recognizing the very real difficulties that children often face by being autistic in an autism-unfriendly world. We view autism as a natural part of humankind, and as such our terminology reflects this unless we are bound by current diagnostic terms that we are required to use clinically.

Neutrality and/or positivity – while retaining levels of honesty

While language should be neutral or positive, there also needs to be an air of honesty involved. While autism per se can be understood in a neutral and positive way, parents may be frustrated if they feel that if their child is struggling so you need to understand that and take that into account. It might be that this is the point where you can introduce the concept of **Autism + Environment = Outcome**. So many parents (and autistic adults) when reframing their understanding within the context of the equation end up with very differing perspectives of autism, as well as sometimes very different ideas as to how to support individuals.

Being autistic *is* very often difficult – because of the environment the child finds themselves in. Many difficulties are shared by the whole family. Ignoring those difficulties would be unfair to the parents, but at the same time moving away from a blame culture (where autism is 'to blame') is likely to be unhelpful in the long term.

Empathy, humility and willingness to learn

Having a sense of being equals, or even for you to put yourself in a position where you can openly suggest that every 'new' autistic child opens up opportunities for learning, can very much earn trust that otherwise might be difficult to gain. Parents will likely appreciate the fact that the pathway to identification is a learning curve not just for them but for you at the same time. The human element of engagement cannot be underestimated.

Making sure that the child is always the focus

Parents are incredibly important – but the most important person in the whole process is the child. Doing everything possible to ensure that no harm is done to the child, including elevated anxiety, is critical. Proactively discussing with parents how best to engage with the child before you ever even meet them is an essential part of the identification pathway. Recognizing that children may often feel anxiety over situations that other children find easy will not only help put measures in place to decrease risk of harm, it is also likely to increase the chances of a trusting relationship between you and the family. As noted in the list above, the discussion around anxiety will already have taken place. Reiterating this at every possible stage can only be a positive aspect of the pathway.

As much work done in advance as possible

Parents are very often extremely busy, and some will have communication requirements that might differ from others. Again, this process will already have started as part of the pathway to identification process, but revisiting it to ensure that time is being used as effectively as possible could help reassure parents that their needs are being respected and taken into consideration. One particular aspect of this might be allowing parents to collate information, prompted by you, in advance of meetings. That way you can take the time to digest the information and come up with follow-up lines of enquiry without having to wait for the information with the parents present. It may well be an effective and efficient pathway.

Location for the process

Families have all sorts of practicalities to take into account, and they are likely to be more complex than your own situation. It is usually more difficult for a whole family to coordinate their activities than it is for a paid professional – having to take time off work, arranging childcare, not being in a position whereby both parents can attend – these are all issues that are unlikely to be an issue for you. Therefore, it makes sense for you to be the one to be as flexible as possible to the family's needs, rather than the expectation always being on them.

Having as many options available to the family as possible can only be of benefit. For example, if the location for discussion could either be at their home, the home of another family member, or your own space, this gives far more flexible permutations than if the family only had one choice. Similarly, being flexible about when the appointment/s could be will make the pathway that much simpler for the family.

Breaking the news

For many parents the moment that you discuss the outcome will be a relief, for some it will simply reiterate what they already knew/suspected – but for some it might come as a shock. For most parents the final decision will cause elevated anxiety and stress. Making sure that prior to the process there is clear guidance as to how, when, and where you will discuss your opinion and in what manner will go some way to reducing that stress, especially if the parents have some say in it. For example, some parents will want a letter sent (or email, or similar) so that they feel that they can react without you there. Some would prefer face-to-face discussion, some will opt for whatever is the quickest way to get the news.

Please avoid any negativity when giving an affirmative decision; rather than 'I'm sorry to say...' you could simply say, 'It is absolutely clear that your child is autistic' – some people advocate the use of terms such as 'congratulations' but this somewhat preempts how parents might be feeling. Note that I have suggested the use of strong language (absolutely clear) – parents do not want to go away wondering whether there is any doubt; parents usually want clarity and certainty.

The time taken for parents to digest and respond (if any response is to be forthcoming) should totally be down to the parents. They may wish to have the decision as their end point of discussion – or, it may be a starting point. Depending on the format of how you break the news all options should be outlined beforehand – for example, if face to face the parents should know that they can ask you to leave them in private, or for them to leave for a chat and then return, or for them to leave and get back in contact with you when they are ready...and any other options that could be available. The key is that there should be as much flexibility as possible for parents.

Report writing

Families will need some level of 'official' documentation that allows them to share their child's identification. It might be useful for you to provide three different pieces of documentation so that parents can choose which one they wish to utilize in different situations. Three options could include:

1 A simple 'official' letter (i.e. with clear letterhead, qualifications, signed) with the confirmed autism identification
2 A summary report which bullet points key aspects of an individual's autistic profile
3 A full report with an in-depth presentation of the child's autistic profile.

The latter might include some or all of the following (the list is not exhaustive!):

- Developmental history
- Full sensory profile
- In-depth communication profile
- Explanation of the child's cognitive profile
- Strengths of the child as well as learning preferences
- An outline of the child's autistic sociality
- Interesting and unusual imagination
- What their spiky profile looks like
- Passionate interests
- Hyper-focus abilities.

Questions I might need answering

- Will my child always be autistic?
- What does this mean for relationships?
- Will she be able to get a job?

- Will he ever be independent?
- Does my child need an intervention?
- Do I need to change my parenting style?

Will my child always be autistic?

The answer to this is yes. But it is more than this – an alternative question that has a darker undertone is, 'Is there a cure for autism?' along with, 'What causes it in the first place?' Your child is born autistic – nothing causes it per se, in as much as what 'causes' a human being – I could go into detail here but I'm sure you know about the facts of life! Of course there are genetic factors involved, and we all now know that vaccines don't suddenly create autistic children. Accepting that your child is autistic and always will be without the rather negative connotations of a cause and/or cure changes the narrative significantly. Rather than seeking a cure for autism, seeking alternative environments to avoid problems and putting one's energy into autistic quality of life seems a better way forward than seeking to irrevocably change a child. One cannot, after all, change a person being autistic.

What does this mean for relationships?

Your child is perfectly capable of having relationships throughout his life; the way in which those relationships develop and with whom will be very much dependent on your child's individual sociality. An autistic sociality is highly likely to be different from that of the PNT, which means in turn that your child is likely to have relationships with different people, possibly in different styles compared to his non-autistic peers. Whether this matters or is anything to be concerned about should stem from your child's preferences. For example, it might be that your child has a fewer number of relationships as friends but the ones she does have are intense and fulfilling; it might also be that those friends are not considered conventional – but, if having an intense and loving relationship with someone from a different age group is what your child craves, and there is nothing inherently 'wrong' with the relationship, then doing things differently is simply that – different, not negative.

In terms of having a long-term partner when your child is older, please don't listen to anyone who suggests that it won't happen. The truth is, no one knows how any child will develop and what their future relationships might look like – and your child, in this sense, is absolutely no different from anyone else. Those who suggest that autistic people can't have rewarding and beautiful relationships with a long-term partner are deluded; ignore anyone who even hints at such scaremongering.

Will she be able to get a job?

As above, the genuine answer is that no one knows. Please avoid listening to people who might try to tell you that it is less likely for autistic people to have successful employment – the absolute, irrefutable fact is that autistic people can and do have fantastic working lives; the goal is to ensure that the child has the best opportunity to be one of those individuals – which could be said of any child. So, as for any child, you will want to encourage interests and skills that lead to future goals (whatever they might be) and don't listen to others who cannot speak on behalf of your child.

Will he ever be independent?

I'm guessing that you will be seeing a pattern here! Again, the answer is 'who knows?' – and the answer to that question is absolutely no one. Nobody has a crystal ball to see your child's future, so no one will have the right to tell you what that future will hold. Just as within the PNT, there are some autistic adults who rely heavily on others for support in various different areas of life, and others who are extremely independent.

While on the subject of independence, it is worth noting that 'being independent' seems to be some kind of grail within society; I am not at all convinced as to the rationale behind this – after all, how many of us really are independent? Almost all of us are dependent on others in all sorts of ways; autistic individuals will also very likely be dependent in some areas and independent in others. Yet again, moving away from what might be conventional and working towards quality of life is highly recommended. Needing to rely on people or systems for things that others might find easy is perfectly acceptable – encouraged, in fact – when it increases quality of life. For example, someone who might find accessing a supermarket stressful might choose to rely heavily on online deliveries; rather than putting a huge amount of energy forcing herself to cope with supermarkets simply because convention states that most people do their shopping in person, recognizing that in the great scheme of things quality of life supersedes having unnecessary skills seems like a very good compromise. The problems arise when society imposes a dictate suggesting that shopping in a supermarket *is* a desired, even necessary independent skill. That level of imposition needs to be avoided at all costs.

Does my child need an intervention?

Many websites will offer 'interventions', and in fact after having done a quick search many of them seem to target parents of children with a recent identification. It is not for me to suggest any sweeping statements around the ethics of this; however, I have included a whole section on interventions in the last chapter so feel free to have a read of that to decide for yourself what the answer to this question might be!

Do I need to change my parenting style?

Well, it rather depends on how you have been parenting up until the point at which you ask the question! Some parents intuitively parent their children in an autism-friendly way before the notion of autism is even considered. However, if, as a parent, you have been 'treating' your child as a PNT then it is highly likely that you will need to adjust your parenting style to make it more suited to your autistic child. Your child, by definition of being autistic, will process the world differently from the PNT – so it makes perfect sense to recognize that the way in which, as a parent, you interact with her, what your expectations are, how you communicate, engage with, play with – could require some level of change compared to a PNT child. In other words, if there really is such a thing as a parenting 'style' it is likely that it will need consideration to ensure that it is best suited to your child.

Don't force parents to parenting classes – do allow for knowledge development

I will be bold and suggest that no parents as a result of their child either being autistic or suspected as being autistic should ever be required to go on a parenting course. Unfortunately, to this day, I know of practice whereby this is a suggestion in some cases, and in others an actual requirement as part of the identification process. To me, this is extraordinarily poor practice for many reasons, including the following.

They don't work

Parenting courses are designed to enable parents to better parent their child, better understand their child, and often to assist parents in learning how to deal with difficult or perceived difficult behaviour. However, if the child is autistic then it is much less likely that the parenting course will be of any use whatsoever – parenting an autistic child is almost always qualitatively different (or should be) from parenting a PNT; their processing styles, by definition, will differ – so what 'works' for one child may very well not work for another.

However, the problem goes even deeper than that – if the assumption is that a child's behaviour is problematic, and going on a parenting course might help to 'solve' that, and the child is, in fact, autistic – then going on a parenting course at best will probably be a waste of time, at worst damaging short and long term for the child and the parents, plus the child will be just as autistic at the end of it as they were at the start. Changing the behaviour of any autistic child bears no relationship whatsoever with them being autistic – I will return to this point when discussing interventions.

The insistence that you go on a parenting course also reinforces that there is something wrong with your parenting skills in the first place. The irony here is that making the assumption that a child is PNT when he is actually autistic, and parenting him in a way that suits the PNT, will increase the chances of you parenting him in a way that is autistically unsuitable. If, on the other hand, you are parenting him in an autism-friendly way – which is highly likely to differ from that of other parents – then you are already doing a good job.

They reinforce that there is something wrong with your child

If the assumption is that you need to change your child in some way by going on a parenting course, the inference is that there is something wrong with the child in the first place. If the 'wrongness' is associated with autism then the message seems to be a clear one – being autistic is to be in the wrong. Such messages have no place whatsoever in this world.

They reinforce normalization

Many parenting courses make the assumption that a perceived 'norm' is a goal – again, the inference being that if your child doesn't fit into this norm then they are somehow in need of changing. This is, essentially, normalization – as above, this has no place in today's society.

In summary, it is very difficult to understand the point of parents being encouraged or forced to go on parenting courses that are not designed specifically for the autistic child. *No parent can make a child autistic by their parenting, no parent can change a child being autistic by their parenting* – there isn't much that is so indefatigable as these statements in relation to parenting!

Knowledge development

While I reject the notion of parenting classes, parents are pretty influential over their children's lives, so are a superb resource in and of themselves. However, being a parent doesn't automatically equate to vast amounts of autism knowledge. No doubt, many parents have extreme levels of expertise around their child – very often, though, this is through their own willingness and determination to develop that expertise independently. Autopia would provide parents with fully funded places on appropriate courses of their choice that are well received within the autism community and recommended by them.

Professional perception/attitudes

It is absolutely essential that the way in which the professional comes across to the parent (and child) is situated firmly within the lens of autism being a perfectly acceptable way of being, while at the same time accepting that being autistic in an autism-unfriendly world can create problems – sometimes, huge problems. Having that combination of absolute acceptance along with a thirsty desire to learn from each and every child, with a dash of fervent desire to combat inequality and best support the family, will go a long way towards developing your relationship with the family – but, even more importantly, influencing the way in which the family thinks about their child, particularly if they are very new to the autism world.

First impressions count – the number of families I know who meet professionals for the first time and are immediately put off them based on the language that they have used, or comments about autism, or similar are too numerous to count. Conversely, if you ask any 'autism family' they will be able to tell you straight away the professionals they have met whom they have trusted – as well as why that is the case, and what an incredibly positive thing it is to have a trusted professional in their lives. I recall a parent bursting into tears on her first contact with a professional. She had phoned him to find out if he might be able to help her son. He spoke to her briefly and then said, 'I am sorry but I need to go soon; I'm meeting an autistic young person and as we know, time can be very important to some folk and I can't risk his distress if I'm late' – she was so overwhelmed at the seemingly innocuous but actually incredibly important appreciation for the autistic way of being that she never forgot; she told me that it was the first time she had ever heard a professional take the 'side' of the autistic child.

The grieving process

I'm not so sure how much this crops up nowadays, but it still comes up more often than it possibly should. Certainly, when I first started learning formally about autism I was told that all parents would naturally go through a grieving process to mourn the fact that their child was autistic. This tragedy model is not one that I subscribe to, and I feel reflects such a lack of autism understanding within society that it deserves no place in it whatsoever. I suspect that the grieving concept is born out of a misplaced belief of what autism is, perpetuated by those who assume that being autistic is synonymous with being intellectually disabled. I don't think that professionals any longer refer to this grieving process. Autopia certainly rejects the notion that one has to grieve a living child.

5

Schools and education

Pros and cons of different schools/ educational environments

Obviously there is a range of provision; this doesn't necessarily mean that the whole range will be available for your child – if only it was as simple as that! It would be an autopian standard without a shadow of a doubt to have a full range of options, all of which were available to all children, but this is such a long way off there needs to be a note of realism as well as optimism. In this chapter, I have listed the most common options available, each with possible issues for your child. Pros and cons are, of course, incredibly individual. Indeed, what might be a pro for one child might be a con for another. I aim to have some level of balance by noting issues that you could consider without necessarily arguing that they are positive or negative per se.

In addition to thinking about which option might be best for your child, there is the issue of how much time is spent in education. For every option listed below there is the added dimension of flexibility around attendance.

Flexi-schooling

Flexi-schooling, where your child learns at school for part of the week and at home for the rest, is an option for your child; however, getting the support of the school is essential if this is an option that you wish to consider. Without the support of the school it can be a difficult path to navigate. There are some really positive aspects of flexi-schooling, though, so it's well worth considering. Some positives include:

- Allowing your child the opportunity to have some level of control
- Acknowledging the finite level of spoons

- Prioritizing motivating learning (style and/or subject)
- Understanding that the educational offer can change reasonably quickly.

Allowing your child the opportunity to have some level of control

Children very rarely have much control or even say over their own educational experience. In light of this, is it even a wonder that so many children find that education fails them? Giving some level of control to the child over how and when they access education (of whatever kind) can make a huge difference, not least to the child's wellbeing. Giving this level of choice often motivates the child to access education *more* than they otherwise would, rather than less, which is often what I hear people say they are concerned about. If you have a child for whom full-time education has led to burnout and, subsequently, to being unable to access education at all, giving the child control over getting back into education often allows them the opportunity to engage at a pace that suits them.

Acknowledging the finite level of spoons

Education can be draining – intellectually, emotionally, physically (due to the sensory environment) and socially. Your child will only have a certain amount of energy each day or week or term; at some point, for many children, full-time education will drain those energy reserves, leaving nothing in the tank. There is literally no point at this stage in accessing education – in fact, a very strong argument could (and should) be made that without a break there could be long-term damage to the child. However, if there is a flexi option in which access to education is based around the levels of finite energy for that day, that week, that term and so on, the more effective that educational process will be. As someone who is interested in triathlons (whereby the spoon analogy is related to burning matches) I am always struck by the notion of the 'perfect race'. The perfect triathlon is one in which by the end of the race the triathlete has burned all her matches, the last one of which goes out on the finish line. This means that the fullest amount of energy has efficiently gone into the race without any wastage but without the triathlete burning out. Having the chance within education to balance one's spoons (or matches) against the energy that accessing education will take can be an effective way of making the most out of education. The added joy of this flexible arrangement, along with the first suggestion of the child having some level of control, is that there will be differing levels of energy matched against different subjects, teachers, environments, ways of teaching and so on. So, for example, a geography lesson for a child might take only half as much energy as a history lesson. Flexibility allows for the child to work out how best to utilize his energy to get the best out of his education.

Prioritizing motivating learning (style and/or subject)

Being in a flexi situation might also allow a child to prioritize those areas of learning in which she can thrive, while avoiding areas that might be problematic (for whatever reason). Too often we assume that this relates to the subject matter itself (e.g. 'I don't like physics') and this may well be the case. Probably, however, it is a little more complex than that. A child might love certain aspects of physics while be less motivated in others; just as importantly, in line with the above, a child might be motivated by things other than the subject itself per se – for example, the way in which it is taught, the classroom it is taught in, or the way in which the subject is assessed. Giving a child some flexible options and subsequently exploring why the choices are being made can be extremely illuminating in terms of how to shape future education to suit a child's motivating factors.

Understanding that the educational offer can change reasonably quickly

Flexi-schooling as an option can be very fluid; if the school is willing then it might be that choices can be made last minute, changes can be made frequently, and the whole educational experience can be far more fluid than the traditional school day/week. For your child this could be invaluable. And remember – less is very often more! I hear the argument against flexi-schooling, usually from teachers, that if a child is missing part of the curriculum then they are missing out. The response to this is to remind ourselves that if a full-time curriculum leads to a complete withdrawal from education due to burnout, then the child ends up not getting any education at all along with an unhealthy dollop of trauma thrown in. If this is the case, then, a reduction in some areas of education actually means in the longer term that the child received more educational opportunities, not fewer.

Mainstream schools

Mainstream schools are, in the main, populated by the PNT. Apologies for pointing out the obvious, but the following points are worth noting as issues to consider in relation to your child.

Reflects many other environments

The argument here is that the closer the educational experience is to 'real life' the better the chances your child will have to learn how to cope in the world, both as a child and as an adult. There is also the argument that your child will have access to PNT peers and be able to learn from them to increase skills that might be deemed to be 'lacking'. It is absolutely the case that mainstream school will, by definition, include plenty of PNT kids; however, this does not necessarily mean that a mainstream environment will equip the child with PNT skills, nor is it necessarily reflective of 'real life'. While most of society's 'environments' are also mostly 'mainstream' there needs to be caution in the philosophy that your child needs to be competent in all of them. After all, your child will not be exposed to all of them and will choose her environment as best she can to suit her needs outside of school and as an adult. The counter-argument to this is that the wider the experiences of your child, and the broader the range of skills he possesses, the more chances he will have to find an environment that suits him.

The reality is that while there *may* be more opportunities in mainstream schools to mingle with the PNT, it does not necessarily mean that your child will develop skills at an intuitive level. Your child has a range of autistic skills, and PNT children have a range of PNT skills. There is subsequently a high expectation on your child to raise his game to fit in with the PNT skill set – which can be extremely tiring for some children, and indeed damaging to others. The section on masking (see later in this chapter) explores this in greater depth. Suffice to say, I am not a fan of trying to somehow get an autistic child to emulate a PNT in order to have more opportunities in life. Whilst it might be hugely advantageous to learn very specific skills (as long as they are not damaging to the child), we are far better off putting our energy into making sure that society has a better autism understanding in order that children can be accommodated.

Finally, in relation to this issue, your child may very well only need to have a specific set of skills as an adult, dependent on what situation he finds himself in. If this is the case, there can be an extraordinary amount of time and energy spent in childhood trying to get a child to develop skills that are unnatural to him 'just in case' he needs them as an adult. Not only might this be a colossal waste of time, he may develop these skills as and when he needs them at a later date anyway, or might never need them at all. It can be draining to the point of damage to always be having to learn skills that are not a natural part of your neurotype, so this kind of direction of travel needs very careful consideration.

Wide range of diverse neurologies

One of the possible benefits of mainstream school is that it is likely to have a wide range of neurodivergent children within it, which may provide a good balance between the ND community and the PNT community. There could be an argument that for all children, the greater the range of ND children they are exposed to and learn from the better – in the case of your child, the argument might be that if it is good practice for PNT children to learn about autism from your child, it is equally good practice for your child to learn about being a PNT from that population.

High academic expectation

Many adults place a great deal of emphasis on academic success at school as it can lead to better opportunities for the future. Mainstream schools are likely to cater for a whole range of academic capabilities, and will often strive for high academic success in terms of pass rates and high grades. This may not be the case in other educational environments. The decision here is how important the academic success or otherwise should be for your child and whether a mainstream school is the best place for her to achieve that.

Large classroom sizes

Many children find large classroom sizes (in terms of population) problematic; this isn't invariably the case, but it does seem an ongoing theme that the smaller, more quiet, and less busy the environment, the less stressful the child will find it. However, as usual, there are always exceptions. There are some children who proactively prefer the potential for anonymity in a more populated environment, for example.

Low level of autism specialism

It is fair to suggest that in mainstream schools there won't be a particularly high level of autism specialism. There will be some level of autism understanding, but this will be incredibly varied, and will differ not just from school to school but from one teacher to the next. Schools have such a wide range of pupil needs that it is often difficult for them to become specialist in any one particular area, and autism is no exception.

Crowded environments

As noted above, mainstream schools are renowned for being busy, crowded, populated places – assembly halls, corridors, classrooms, canteens and play areas are all likely to be full of pupils. This can be a positive for some, and a negative for others – either way, your child's preferences will need to be taken into consideration.

Wide-ranging opportunities for extra-curricula activities

Many mainstream schools, as a direct result of the range of pupils within them, will have a wide-ranging selection of extra-curricula activities, including lunch clubs and after-school activities. If you find a school that caters specifically for your child's passionate interest then it could be the single most important deciding factor for their education.

Resource-attached schools

Resources attached to a mainstream school are an option in some cases, where the school feels that a child might need to access a slightly more specialized environment but will still benefit from some of the mainstream opportunities. Issues to consider include the following.

Access to mainstream

Having access to all that mainstream offers but within what might be seen as a safe (or safer) haven of a resource attached to a mainstream school could be seen as a positive option. However, do make investigations before making any decisions. Some resources are way better than others at engaging with the mainstream aspects of education, whereas others are sometimes essentially an alternative provision that makes little or no use of any advantages that mainstream might have to offer.

Higher level of expected autism understanding

You cannot rely on this, but there is a higher chance of there being a better level of autism understanding within an attached resource. Staff are more likely to be better trained, have more experience, and very often be more motivated to work with autistic children than in mainstream. Very often staff will have trained to be teachers without considering that there will be an expectation that they will be teaching ND children. While it may not be an issue for lots of staff, there may be some teachers who find this extremely difficult. Teaching staff know that within attached resources they will be engaging with autistic children and proactively choose to do so, therefore it seems reasonable to suggest that there is a greater motivation from those staff which could lead to higher levels of understanding. It might even be the case (though I cannot prove this) that there are a higher number of ND teaching staff in non-mainstream environments.

Smaller classroom sizes

Again, this isn't always a given, but it could be that classes are smaller in number within a resource. As noted above – this might be beneficial for your child, or bring its own issues.

Higher staffing ratio

Another one for which there is no hard and fast rule, but the chances are that staffing may be at a higher level than within mainstream. Again, this might be a positive for your child – but higher staffing also has its drawbacks. Some children find that high staff ratios make them feel crowded, in the spotlight, and cramped whereas an atmosphere with fewer staff makes them feel more relaxed and less anxious.

Potential for othering

Any 'split' from a mainstream environment, especially one which is attached to a mainstream school, increases the risk of othering the children who attend it. This is not the fault of the resource per se, but is one of those perennial issues when it comes to all areas of life, not just education. If a child is in need of a differing type of support (in this case education) and that support cannot be found within a mainstream school, then is a resource attached to a mainstream school a good example of inclusion, despite the fact it is deliberately taking the child out of the mainstream environment, or does it perpetuate the notion of 'other'? I have written more on the nature of inclusion later, but in this instance we should not fall into the trap of assuming that inclusion and integration are synonymous, nor that providing differing types of support is poor practice.

Similar academic possibilities

One of the benefits of a resource attached to a mainstream school is that it has access to essentially the same academic opportunities as the mainstream counterpart. Technically, all education should have the same access, but in reality the practicalities (such as access to equipment, teaching knowledge, resources) will differ in schools that have fewer children accessing a mainstream curriculum.

Special schools

A generic special school will usually cater for children with additional learning disabilities. They often have higher numbers of autistic children compared to mainstream school. Issues for consideration include the following.

Higher level of specialism

Whilst it is fairly reasonable to suggest that a special school (i.e. a school catering for a range of needs) will have a higher degree of specialisms, including autism, it by no means equates to them all having the skills and abilities to understand your child. Never make that assumption!

Wide range of needs

With a diverse range of children will come a wide range of needs; presumably, this could increase the likelihood of the school being in a position to suit your child, but it is no certainty. Much depends – obviously – on the needs of your child. An autistic child can be of any intellectual and academic ability, so much depends on what curriculums the school provides, what skills they have to teach varying intellectual abilities, and where your child fits in (or doesn't) to all of these.

Higher staff ratios

It is very likely that special schools will have higher staff ratios compared to mainstream schools. There is often the assumption that the more the merrier applies when it comes to staffing but this may not necessarily be the case. Under-staffing causes massive problems – but so can the rarer over-staffing. However, if your child is more secure in an environment in which there is a higher staff:student ratio then this might be something you need to consider.

Lower academic expectations

Some special schools may have lower academic expectations and may not be used to taking students who are potentially high achievers. If your child has the academic capability of a high achiever then this may be problematic for you.

Autism-specific schools

Some schools are set up to cater only for autistic children. The following points are worth noting as issues to consider if you are thinking about this type of setting.

Supposed high level of specialism

Note that I have put 'supposed' – just because a school claims specialism doesn't automatically make it specialist! All schools will vary in terms of their skills and abilities in understanding autism – none of this matters, what does matter is what understanding a school has of your child!

Access to peers

Having an environment in which all children are autistic can have its advantages for some children. Feeling safe and 'at home' within a school setting because you are part of a community as well as having some overlapping needs with peers can be a delight for some children.

Varying academic expectations

Many specialist schools will have systems in place to cover broader curricula than other settings; however, unless the school can offer an academic curriculum that is of the standard your child needs it might be a problem.

Potential for far greater flexibility

While never a guarantee, there is at least a chance that a highly specialist school will be more flexible to meet autistic need than the average mainstream. If your child requires high levels of adaptations that within a mainstream environment are not considered to be reasonable adjustments, then it might be that an autism-specific school would be able to better meet those needs.

Different set of policies

I have written briefly about policies in the last chapter, but suffice to say here that mainstream policies that are aimed at the PNT may not be suitable for your child. A specialist school with the autistic child at the centre of the stage should have policies that are far more suitable.

Possible transport support

While not always the case, many specialist schools have an understanding that transport can be a problem for many children, and aim to work with parents and local authorities to work out the best way of getting children to and from school. This way of working isn't exclusive to specialist provision but I suspect that it is more likely than within most mainstream environments.

Home education

At present you are perfectly entitled to home educate your child, and yet you are not entitled to any of the funding that would have been allocated to a school should your child have accessed it. This seems wrong to me; home education for some children is an absolute joy, and can be a total game changer. I would not advocate it for all children, but if school is causing so much distress that a child needs to seek solace at home, then home education could be a genuinely positive and life-affirming option. I don't buy into the arguments that it isolates the child, takes away their access to peers and the like – just because a child is home educated doesn't mean that they are suddenly cut off completely from society! There are often very healthy and well-run home education networks that provide all sorts of opportunities for children in a home education setting that can fulfil social and education opportunities. Autopia would support the notion of home education being funded as well as investment in how home-educated children and their families can best be supported.

In a similar vein, as the Covid-19 pandemic has demonstrated, there can be all sorts of educational activity of a high quality accessible online. Autopia very much aligns with the idea that accessing virtual environments while in a safe space (in this case home) could be a superb option for some children. More investment and understanding are needed around how to create more fluid arrangements that include online learning for those for whom it is a best fit.

Yurts/rivers/forests/alternative venues

Being educated at a school or at home should not be the only options available for your child. We need more educational environments that can suit a variety of needs – forest schools, yurts, outdoor teaching – all of these are examples of different ways of teaching that have the potential to change the way in which children learn for ever.

Autistic teachers

Not all autistic teachers make for great teachers of autistic children – but having more autistic teachers available to increase the chances of being cognitively aligned with their students can only be a positive. Autopia recognizes that there may need to be adjustments made in how teacher training is run in order to attract more autistic adults who may have a lot to offer the teaching profession.

Things to consider when choosing a school

Class size

The size of your child's class could be of extreme importance. Does she prefer a very calm, quiet environment with as few people within it as possible? Does he prefer a busier environment in which it is easier to be less conspicuous?

Staff knowledge and attitude (including leadership)

I suppose it should go without saying, but autism knowledge is something that really needs investigating as part of your journey to choosing the best fit school. This might be easier said than done! You might not need to have the entire school's staff to have excellent autism credentials – it might be that a smaller number of key staff along with excellent support systems will be absolutely fine. Much of what happens in education for children will depend on what the general atmosphere and attitude is within the staff team, which will often reflect the leadership team.

Don't fall into a trap of thinking that a good programme of training and/or qualifications will automatically lead to a good school for your child. Much will depend on the training, the course, what content there is, how much staff have listened, understood, taken on board; they might have had the best training in the world but if they are not supported to change by their leadership team it may make little difference. Staff may have academic qualifications with the word autism in the title, but if the courses do not align with an appropriate understanding of autism (and what support children might require) then it might be worse than having no qualifications at all.

Knowledge and understanding of autism are so important and – yes – it is more likely that training and qualifications will have a positive impact, but it cannot be a guarantee.

Transition planning

If the school doesn't have a very clear, autism-friendly plan to allow pupils to transition into it at a pace suited to them then I would suggest that it should ring at least an alarm bell or two. It is highly likely that your child will need more support to transition into a new environment compared to the PNT, so if a school doesn't recognize the need for a transition plan then I would question whether staff really do have the requisite knowledge of autism to be able to competently meet your child's needs.

Willingness to listen and be flexible

This might sound a little obvious, but you may be surprised at the number of schools that claim they know how to support a child because they have had previous experience. I always worry about this as another red flag – surely assuming one understands autistic children just because one has worked with them before is essentially an acknowledgement that one *doesn't* genuinely understand autism! You will be able to pick up very quickly whether staff at a school are more of the open-minded ilk who genuinely want you to share information about your child and work alongside you to ascertain what a child's support needs might be, rather than those who claim to already know it all.

Length of school day

The length of the school day varies across schools and could be something that you need to consider carefully. Start times, duration, and finish times along with what breaks there are available are all aspects that could influence your child's experiences.

The more flexible the school is in negotiating such things with you the better!

Location/transport

As with the duration of the school day, this is an area that sometimes gets overlooked. There are too many examples of children who are basically wrecked emotionally and mentally before they even arrive at school as a result of the transport they are required to take to get there. If travel plays a key part in your child's energies then the location of the school and how she will get there (and back) need careful consideration.

Current number of pupils who could be regarded as ND

This is not something that will necessarily be a 'game changer' but it is always worth finding out whether the school has a history of high numbers of ND children as a natural part of its development. Some of the best schools I have known are not schools that promote themselves in any way as schools for neuro-diversity, but due to their nature they have attracted ND children to the point that the ND population is extremely high.

The sensory environment

Perhaps this should go without saying, but the sensory environment will have an impact on your child; the question is, will a specific school environment impact positively overall or negatively? Does the school automatically ask for a sensory profile of your child to ascertain what might need changing – if not, why not? I have included a more detailed section on sensory later, but it is essential that sensory issues are taken into consideration when making a choice around school placement.

Policies

All schools will have various policies, and it might be useful to ask for access to key ones such as inclusion, behaviour, and bullying to work out for yourselves whether they feel autism-friendly. I have gone into more detail around what good policy might look like below – but remember, those versions are autopian ones to work towards rather than ones to expect in the current climate. However, it is still worth finding out if school policies habitually and genuinely take neurodiversity into account in a way that would suit your child.

Autopia standards

This section goes through just some of the key elements of school life that autopia holds dear. So, these are ideas that I feel would benefit children – and, in fact, not just autistic children but all children. Maybe some of the practice outlined below is already happening, but much of it is practice that educationalists could work towards. To reiterate – these ideas stem from autistic experiences shared with me; so, while not evidenced-based as such, they do have some level of rationale behind them.

Teaching and learning

Teaching of authistory and neurodivershistory

Imagine what it would be like if there was a statutory requirement to teach the history of autism and neurodiversity as an ongoing core subject throughout education. I feel that primary-aged children are often best suited to the ideas of what constitutes difference, as they are often young enough not to have developed bias themselves, and old enough to absorb very useful life lessons, so maybe much of authistory and neurodivershistory could be taught throughout primary school with follow-up ongoing lessons in secondary. The curriculum for these core subjects should be written by autistic adults and validated amongst the autistic community and evaluated and updated by the autistic community as new concepts around those subjects emerge.

So – an autopian vision includes:

1 A small group of autistic academics design what is to be taught.
2 The same group develop all of the teaching materials across a range of ages and abilities.

3 All materials and resources are available for a wide consultation within the autistic community for agreement.

4 An ongoing core group of autistic individuals who are available for consultation for individual schools around advice for delivery.

5 The same core group are tasked with maintaining the resources and curriculum, updating it when necessary, and cascading those changes across education.

6 A pool of autistic adults on the payroll to provide schools with individual perspectives as part of the ongoing programme.

The outcomes of integrating such programmes into the everyday educational activity, rather than having an 'autism awareness day' or similar, cannot be discounted. The autopian vision is that neurodiversity becomes a part and parcel of everyday life, with an accurate understanding of its history, what the flaws were (and, in fact, are) as regards to autistic community and how autistic people are understood, and how thinking has evolved over the years.

In order that neurodiversity is not seen as some kind of 'add-on', autopia supports the idea of broader diversity curricula being developed, within which the above subjects can sit. If education, as a natural, ongoing part of everyday life, tackled societal issues around minority groups and diversity head on, it might decrease the chances of poor practice and create an ethos of acceptance of difference.

The ethics of difference

In line with the above, education can teach about the ethics of difference; what being 'different' actually means, the positives of diversity within society, case studies of historical and contemporary figures who have added to society who might be regarded as 'different' in some way.

Autodidactic learning

Many children have different learning styles, and many will be good autodidactic learners. There are currently limited opportunities for children within education to learn in diverse ways;

there is usually a traditional way of teaching and learning that all children are expected to engage with. However, autopia recognizes that with a diverse population there will likely be a diverse range of learning styles, and these should be taken into account to best suit the educational needs of individual students. If it became common practice for pupils to choose which type of activity they prefer in relation to a particular aspect of teaching, it would increase the chances for students who might struggle otherwise.

For example, a school might encourage all of the following:

- A quiet area for students to access along with support materials to learn independently
- Study areas for small groups of students to work alongside each other
- Classrooms with more traditional teacher-led activities
- Online options.

These varied options come with all sorts of pragmatic issues – remember, this is an autopian vision, not something that is likely to be put into practice overnight! The main point, though, is that if learning styles vary, then without a variety of different opportunities it is likely that some pupils will be at a disadvantage. Conversely, the more varied the options available, the less risk there is of discrimination.

All exams offered with alternatives when possible

The way in which student knowledge is assessed does need attention, of that I am absolutely convinced. Not all pupils will excel at exams which, by definition, means that if exams are the only way of assessing knowledge then those young people will be at a disadvantage. The current system is extremely limited – I suspect more due to workloads and the immense pressure on the education system than anything else – but looking to an autopian future, there needs to be a range of options to assess knowledge to accurately reflect student ability in a subject area, as opposed to a student's ability to take an exam.

All exams accredited by an autistic panel of teachers

For children who do wish to take exams, it would be useful for exam questions to be assessed for suitability by a panel of autistic teachers. I don't know of any current practice that habitually does this, but without due care and attention there is a risk of discrimination if exam questions are set in such a way that make the process harder for autistic processing.

Emphasis on coursework and different formats for coursework

Some children would choose individual coursework over a period of time to demonstrate their subject knowledge as opposed to one or two exams, so this should be an option for a child. There should also be different options for how the coursework can be presented. For example, a piece of work could be a written piece or a presentation – even giving the option here of a presentation doubles the choice for a student!

Pupil choice of assessments

Having a level of student choice over how they wish to be assessed might seem a bold suggestion, and yet there is so much rhetoric over the 'student voice' within, for example, EHCPs. If we really mean it, then we should put it into action. There is a whole variety of ways in which we can assess an individual's knowledge, some of which will be more accurate than others dependent on the learner; why, then, shouldn't we take the individual student's voice into account when working out how best to judge knowledge? Again, this increases all sorts of workloads – but, if education is about learning, and subsequently if we want to genuinely find out what education has taught students, then we should be doing all we can to accurately teach and assess.

Policies and attitudes

Behaviour policies can be hugely problematic when it comes to their application to children. If they are written with the PNT in mind (and, presumably, in the main they are) then their application without taking autism into account could be damaging to the child. One of the most common problems with such policies is the language that is used and the subsequent interpretation of that language when applied to any given individual. For example, a behaviour policy might state 'a zero tolerance to rude, inappropriate, or disruptive behaviour'. The issue with this statement is that it is pretty much entirely open to interpretation. Not only that, but if that interpretation is not within an autism-lens context then a child may easily fall foul of the policy simply by being autistic. The concepts of rudeness, inappropriateness and disruptive are negotiable, fluid and contextual. They are not rigid, absolute and concrete, and this can give rise to children being unfairly treated to the point of exclusion, simply by being naturally autistic. What a PNT teacher feels is rude is another child's trustworthy honesty. What is a PNT teacher's version of inappropriate is another child's natural appropriateness. What is a PNT teacher's version of disruptive is another child's sensory necessity.

In order for policies to sit within the Equality Act they need very careful consideration. My view is that terms as noted above are so ambiguous and open to interpretation that there is a risk of autistic pupils being at a substantial disadvantage as a result. If this is, indeed, the case, then a reasonable adjustment could well be a careful re-write of the policy with the caveat that autistic pupils need to be understood within their autism lens, rather than the policy being applied as if they were PNT.

The need for autism-specific or even autistic-specific policies

Policies not only need to take autism into account, they may also need to take individual children into account. This might seem like an onerous task – but the alternative might be that a child is extremely unfairly treated. Which is easier to accept – some preventative low-level additional work to understand a child, or to unfairly punish her due to ignorance? We know that exclusion rates are ridiculously high for children, and we also know that many of those exclusions are based on behaviour. What we don't know is how many of those exclusions stem from an overly rigid behaviour policy and/or a lack of understanding of a child being naturally autistic. It is essential, if we want children to be fairly treated, that individual autism-related ways of being are understood and, when appropriate, accepted within ordinary school life – if these contravene a behaviour policy set up for the PNT then all staff need to be aware. For example, if a behaviour policy states that 'all students must be mindful of each other and cause no disruption in class' and yet Charlie, the autistic student, *needs* to stim in order to be able to focus, then this needs to be taken into account. Allowing Charlie to sit at the back of the class so he is out of the eyeline of other students might be a simple solution – what is not an appropriate solution is to punish him for his autistic way of learning.

Reconceptualization of what constitutes good behaviour

There needs to be a broader understanding as to what 'good behaviour' even looks like. Or even if it can really be seen. Take two children in class. One looks attentive, sitting still, looking at the teacher. The other is looking out of the window, twiddling his fidget toy, and rocking on his chair. It might appear that one child is behaving well while the other isn't. In reality the first child is thinking about what his gaming activity might be later on that day, while the second child is doing what he needs to do in order to focus on what the teacher is saying.

Behaviour in general – and, more specifically, at school – really needs a massive rethink or else we will continue to disadvantage autistic pupils. Only ever viewing behaviour through a PNT lens is highly likely to hugely increase risk of misunderstanding the communicative intent of the autistic pupil; more often than not they will end up in a situation, often out of their control, within which the punishment is directed at them and their family.

Recognition that all behaviour is communication

There is a tendency at school for behaviour to be reacted to – sometimes, rather instinctively. All behaviour is a form of communication – the trick is to understand what is being communicated. Taking time out to reflect on behaviour and ascertain what might have prompted it is always going to be better than an immediate reaction. If a child is behaving in a way that is natural to them, then they should never be sanctioned for it. It might be that a particular behaviour is problematic – but that doesn't mean that the child should be punished for it.

If a child is in distress and she can see no easy way out of a situation then she will go into fight, flight, or freeze mode. This will usually appear at a behavioural level that if only understood from a behaviour perspective may very well seem problematic. Take the child who is in freeze mode – which is likely to be a shutdown. Not responding to questions, not being compliant, not following instructions – these are all examples of how a shutdown might be interpreted, when in fact he is at crisis point. Similarly, fleeing a situation – again, because she is in crisis – is seen as absconding. I have written a little more on behaviour later – but in the meantime, autopia follows the following principles:

- Behaviour terms such as 'challenging' are replaced with 'distressed'
- Schools understand that if a child hits genuine crisis point then they have very little, if any, control over their behaviour
- Behaving in a naturally autistic way should not be punished
- Behaviour must always be understood through that child's autistic lens
- Every effort must be made to avoid a child having to hit crisis
- It is the school's responsibility as much as the child's to engage in a way that suits everyone.

Behaviour terms such as 'challenging' are replaced with 'distressed'

If terms are changed – for example challenging behaviour is known as anxiety-induced or distressed behaviour – then there is a very different feel to the phrase. On the one hand there is a blame culture around the child, on the other there is an acceptance that very often behaviour that is deemed problematic is as a direct result of high degrees of anxiety and distress – so, if those negative emotional states are being experienced at school, then it stands to reason that there is a problem with how school is supporting the child, and subsequently a responsibility to do something urgent about it.

Schools understand that if a child hits genuine crisis point then they have very little, if any, control over their behaviour

Children do not like having meltdowns; it can be a deeply disturbing and emotionally draining experience. Many autistic adults will report feeling out of control when they are in this state (and I include flight and freeze in this too). What we simply must never do is have expectations that are absolutely beyond the child's capabilities at that point of crisis, nor should there be any shaming of those children after a meltdown has occurred.

Just imagine, if you will, that you are being exposed to an audience – for example you are speaking at a big conference and you are unused to public speaking. You are highly anxious, and as a result forget words, repeat yourself, lose track of what you are saying, make a total mess of the presentation and basically barely get through an horrendous situation. Would you then think it fair if those around you insisted on going through every mistake that you'd made and ensured that the shame you already felt was amplified, made as public as possible – and then, finally, you were punished for it? This is not even as bad an experience as many individuals report had happened to them as pupils at school following a crisis. The level of blame and shame, the level of accountability for actions they couldn't control, is staggering. This has to stop, otherwise we will continue traumatizing our children to devastating ends.

Behaving in a naturally autistic way should not be punished

As noted elsewhere, being autistic will mean that one is very likely to behave in ways that are not considered 'traditional' – and this should never be punished. See the section on interventions for more detail.

Behaviour must always be understood through that child's autistic lens

Not only must we understand a child through *the* autism lens, we must understand her through *her* autism lens. Every child will have different reasons for their behaviour, and it is important to recognize that just because two autistic children display the same behaviour, we must never make the assumption that the reason behind that behaviour is invariably the same for both of them.

Every effort must be made to avoid a child having to hit crisis

This is a big one! When I wrote a book on anxiety I thought at the start that it would be all about supporting autistic children to be less stressed. By the end of it I realized that actually, the book is really aimed at everyone else to reduce anxiety on behalf of the child – this is because, in the main, it is external environmental factors that cause so much anxiety, so the fairest and best way of reducing anxiety for the child is to remove the source of it in the first instance. Autopia suggests that it is the school as a whole that is required to examine all areas of potential anxiety-inducement and do whatever is needed to reduce or eliminate causes of anxiety.

It is the school's responsibility as much as the child's to engage in a way that suits everyone

As noted above, it is the school's responsibility to identify the best way to engage with your child. Far too often the responsibility to adapt and 'conform' is down to the child, as opposed to school systems adapting and changing for your child. It might seem daunting to expect a school to change whole school systems, seemingly for a small number of pupils – but in the main autism-friendly systems will very much suit *all* children, so an autopian school system could well be the best fit for everyone.

Reward charts and similar

Charts for behaviour and/or achievement can be unfair and stigmatizing. Charts for 'good sitting' or 'good writing' or 'good attention' that are on view for the whole class can be massively distressing for the child who needs to wriggle due to sensory issues, finds writing nigh on impossible because of her proprio-ception, and is always deemed inattentive simply because she doesn't look at the teacher when he is speaking. That child might be the best learner in the class and yet consistently gets publicly shamed on a daily basis.

Autopia encourages the school to work out what it is they are really rewarding. If children are being rewarded for masking and fitting in and forcing themselves to be more like the PNT then there is something very wrong indeed. In general, children need to be understood and accepted, not rewarded to be more like the PNT.

Sensory

Schools need to take the child's sensory profile into account. It's as simple as that. Not taking it into account and/or not making reasonable adjustments are not only unlawful and discriminatory, they can be extremely harmful for the child and damaging to their education. In some cases it will be the deciding factor for a child being educated in school or not. In other cases (and these are real examples) an inappropriate sensory environment might mean a child cannot access basic needs such as going to the toilet, or eating. That is how important the sensory environment might be.

A child should never be exposed to a sensory environment which causes them undue stress, so it is important that a child has an appropriate sensory profile that can be matched against the school environment before ever setting foot in the facility. Or, more accurately, the school environment needs an appropriate assessment against the child's sensory profile to make sure that it is suitable.

The following is a list of potential sensory issues with an autopian suggestion for how to address them.

School uniforms

Almost all schools have school uniforms and it is totally understandable why this is the case. However, having a school uniform does not mean that the uniform comes in a one size fits all manner (excuse the pun). Uniforms could have a variety of options to ensure that a child's sensory needs are met. The following are autopian suggestions on how to tackle some of the issues with school uniform.

- **Every single item must have an alternative:** Whatever the item of clothing, there must be alternatives available – so, rather than one school polo shirt, a variety of options should be available with various different shapes and materials. This must include any clothing that is required at school, including the PE kit.

- **Ban ties or change rules:** Some children will find having to wear a tie hugely problematic, to the point of feeling that they can't breathe properly. My autopian perspective is that ties are banned altogether as an outdated and unnecessary accessory; however, in the meantime, if ties are imperative then the rules around wearing them should be relaxed. For example, students should *not* have to do up a top button and ties can be a clip-on if needs be. As regards the former suggestion, I have come across some people in education who insist that all students wear button shirts with a tie and that the top button *must* be fastened. I am yet to understand what this has to do with education.
- **Allow different footwear:** Many children will find shoes immeasurably problematic – getting the right footwear can be a frightening prospect for a child, and parents reading this may well be wryly nodding at this stage (or running for the hills in despair). If there is the added school insistence narrowing the choice it can literally be the final straw for the child.

The autopian uniform

It's a useful concept to promote the fact that the more variety there is, the more choice a child has, the less likely they will be discriminated against. Having a range of 'uniforms' and making it the norm that children will have a variety of preferences can alleviate some of the sensory issues that a child may face. For example, I adore the idea of a school onesie, which includes teachers who find it comfortable teaching in them along with some of their students.

Assembly

Some children will simply find assemblies too sensorially overwhelming to access. The very nature of being in a very crowded environment, often with poor acoustics, with all the variety of smells and sounds – it can all add up to the assembly experience being negative for the child. The autopian alternative is to be as inclusive as possible; find a way of attending without attending – in this day and age it should be easy for a child to be in a quiet, safe space and to 'dial in' to such an event that is being live streamed. That way he doesn't have to miss out on the assembly nor does he have to suffer from having to be there in person. Just as an aside, here – forcing a child to go to an assembly that is overwhelming for him doesn't do anyone any favours at all. As he is very unlikely to actually glean anything useful from the experience if his senses are overwhelmed there really is no point to him being there. At the very least it will be forcing him into an uncomfortable situation that he cannot learn from, and at worst it will cause all sorts of problems that could lead to trauma.

Clocks

Ticking clocks can be a distraction that is wholly unnecessary. Replacing clocks along with any other noises that might cause an issue is a positive idea. Digital clocks, for example, are way less distracting.

No school bell

It should be a relatively simple thing to get rid of school bells in the main – many school bells are astonishingly hideous from an auditory perspective at the best of times; if one is noise sensitive then the school bell can literally be a physical assault on the senses. Being exposed to such physical abuse is clearly wrong, so if school bells can be replaced with alternative systems of communication then we should be doing what we can in order to make those changes. Even changing the noise of the school bell to something less harsh is a better alternative to most school bells; eliminating them altogether when possible is an even better solution. Bells to indicate the beginning and end of lessons at the very least could be removed; I am sure that teaching staff are perfectly capable of coordinating their time keeping and ending their lesson on time without needing to rely on a noise that has the potential to harm a child.

Transitions between lessons

The corridor crush is a situation that children are far too often exposed to. If one is tactile sensitive then such times can be traumatic indeed. One solution might be that children stay in the same classroom (where possible; there are some lessons that require a change in environment) and teaching staff take responsibility for moving between classes rather than the responsibility being on the students. This has the added benefit of being able to match individual classes with the sensory needs of those children within them. Another possibility is to have longer transition times to include quiet transitions, when those vulnerable to trauma have the opportunity to transition safely in smaller numbers.

Finding places in school

Some children may find it excessively difficult to find their way around school. Please don't fall into the trap of thinking that they will 'get used to it'; some children may indeed find it easier after being at the school for a while, but don't underestimate the fear of being lost for those children on that literal journey. Unless you have experienced the genuine fear of being lost you won't be able to empathize – just have faith that it is a very scary place to be and should be avoided at all costs. Some children will never learn to find their way around school – much like someone who is colour blind who, however hard they try, will never 'see' colour in any different way. People who cannot recognize faces (prosopagnosia) can't force themselves to suddenly not have prosopagnosia. A child with no sense of direction cannot will themselves into being a skilled navigator – trust me, if they could, then they would!

Autopia suggests that all schools should have systems to support navigation. Clear arrows to all venues and/or colour-coded indicators can make a huge difference. Think about areas that are renowned for being difficult to navigate such as large hospitals, and how useful it is to have a clear system within them that you can rely on to find where you need to be. Then imagine that you can't rely on that system and are left to your own devices to find your way around, and how that makes you feel. Providing directional support around schools is an inexpensive way to alleviate anxiety – why would we not do it?

Safe eating spaces

Children need to eat. This sounds like such a basic premise that it's hardly worth noting – wrong! You may be astonished at the number of reports I hear about children being denied spaces that suit them in order to be able to eat in safety, or even eat at all. The sensory environment of the school canteen can be calamitous to a child with sensory sensitivities. The noises and smells alone can be enough to exclude the child. Added to that are children with issues around seeing other people masticate, issues around being watched while eating, needing to eat in a very specific environment – it is not at all uncommon for this part of school life to be a hidden but poisonous arena that children need protecting from.

Autopia allows children to have access to the space that they require to be able to eat in peace. This might need to be a solitary activity, or outdoors, or sat in the school minibus! Whatever the space, it is provided. By the way – to those people who suggest that it is unhealthy or unsafe to eat outdoors because of inclement weather, I would respond by suggesting that appropriate clothing and eating outdoors is far healthier than a child not being able to eat.

Typing not writing

I've written about this elsewhere, but I can't help repeating my own words, such is the importance of the message. For children with difficulty with fine motor coordination (proprioception) who find holding a pen painful, typing not writing needs to be their mantra. Forcing a child to hand write when typing is a perfectly acceptable alternative is very possibly discriminatory and unlawful.

No adverse lighting

One of the most common stereotypes around the sensory side of autism is that children cannot abide strip lighting. I have no idea how prevalent this actually is, but I do know that for those who find strip lighting a problem, it can be a very major problem indeed – both the flickering of the lights (not usually picked up by the PNT unless the light is on its way out) and the ticking noise they make (again, usually only processed by the PNT when the light is at its end of life). Autopia has lighting that is uplifted/ refracted (so no direct lights in the room) along with individual spotlights for this who like direct light. All lighting has dimmer switches, and each individual light has its own dimmer, so that there is maximum control over lighting within all rooms. Strip lighting is strictly banned!

No fire alarms

The fire alarm going off is meant to be alarming – I guess the clue is in the name! However, the fire alarm is also meant to keep people safe. If one's response to a fire alarm going off is to flee it without any regard as to where one is going, or it immobilizes you such is the sensory onslaught, then it might be counter-intuitive. If a school includes a child for whom the fire alarm elicits such reactions then it is a priority safety issue to seek an alternative. One alternative is to have a visual rather than auditory system, for example having emergency flashing lights as opposed to emergency sirens if it complies with safety guidelines.

Vestibular equipment as standard

Some children will crave vestibular stimulation as part of their sensory needs. Some children will crave movement of one kind or another to enable their learning to be as effective as possible. I find it extraordinary that some children are told to sit still *within a learning environment* when sitting still reduces the opportunity to learn. Children with the need to move should absolutely be given the opportunity to do so. I don't for one second buy into this idea that it would be disruptive for the class; I teach students frequently within environments that allow for movement and I've not had any issues arising. The point is that movement for some children is a necessary part of learning; to limit it is to limit their learning which kind of defeats the purpose of education.

Other children may seek vestibular movement at certain times during the day away from the class, for example needing to use the trampoline every couple of hours. Again, I have heard arguments against this – for example, if a child is not in the classroom then he's not learning; the reality is that those few minutes spent on the trampoline *aid* learning – without it the child may not be learning at all.

Autopia has myriad vestibular equipment accessible to all children who need it, and it is such a common part of education that no one sees it as unusual when a child takes herself off to have a go on the rocking horse (or similar).

Additional school issues

Safe spaces

The need for safe spaces cannot be underestimated. It is imperative that your child knows exactly how to find a safe space and be allowed to go to it when needed. If a child is feeling unsafe then it is essential that they can remove themselves from the situation in order to find their safe space. What this space looks like will very much depend on the child. For some it may not be a physical space, it might be access to a person, or a phone call, or a trusted peer.

It is astonishing to me that schools often fail to accept that a child in distress can often know that they are in distress and can (and should) make the decision to remove themselves from that situation to seek safety. It should be of paramount importance that a child should feel safe as much as is humanly possible within school; denying a child that right, indeed not doing everything possible to ensure that that right is fully addressed, is hugely problematic. So many children are put on programmes to keep them where they are expected to be (i.e. within class) which only adds to their distress. A combination of safe spaces plus ongoing investigations as to why the child is in distress in the first instance is infinitely better than forcing a child to suppress their fear and remain in a distressing situation. So frequently it is the case that those around the child simply do not understand why the child is in distress. I can absolutely see why it might be difficult for people to not understand – but this is absolutely no excuse to assume there is not a problem. Not being able to see the problem or understand it doesn't make the problem go away!

Autopia recognizes the need for all children to feel safe, or to have the opportunity to seek safety when they need to do so. All children are encouraged to self-regulate – in other words to ascertain for themselves when they are in a position of fight, flight, or freeze and to take appropriate action to remove themselves from those situations in order to feel safe.

Homework

It is commonly known that homework is no fun for most children – but, for some, it is seemingly an impossibility. Some children simply cannot tolerate homework. If this is the case then it must be recognized that additional work outside school hours needs to be presented in a way that is acceptable to the child. Before- and after-school spaces to complete work and dedicated time during breaks can be offered as an alternative, for example.

Group work

Some children find that working as part of a group can be so anxiety-inducing that it's simply not fair to force them into doing it. I absolutely understand the argument that children 'need' to learn how to work as a group, that teamwork is important, that no one can go through life completely on their own. However, I also absolutely understand that autistic wellbeing is essential – the very basic yet fundamental concept that mental wellbeing should be a priority for all children is one that should trump the 'need' for group work. The idea that teamwork skills are more important than mental health is ludicrous. The real issue here is that many people simply don't understand the potential negative impact that things like group work pose to some children.

Having additional options available is, of course, the way forward. Individual work alongside group work could be an option for all children – after all, variety is sometimes a good thing.

Break times/lunchtimes

If your child is one for whom mixing with others is problematic, then she needs an alternative to breaks and lunch times that avoid the necessity of engaging with others (see safe spaces).

PE/sports

Sport is an area that some children may excel in, but others might find it hugely problematic. Sometimes it is the sport itself, but there may be other factors to consider. Autopia suggests consideration of the following:

- A choice of sports: as is a common theme in autopia, the more choice available the more likely it is that a child will find something that is suitable to them. Team sports may be rejected in favour of more individual pursuit (e.g. a child choosing athletics over rugby).
- Particular attention to sensory needs: the clothing that is required needs just as much consideration as the school uniform – children's sensory system doesn't switch off just because it's a PE lesson!
- Washing: some children find the idea of having to shower in a group, or even get changed as part of a crowd, terrifying. As noted above – the child's mental wellbeing is important, here and throughout education (and beyond). Having PE at the end of the day might be an option so that children can go home to wash.
- Opting out: if PE/sports are so distressing to a child and an alternative that suits him cannot be found then there should always be the option of opting out.

Training for schools

Remember – this is an autopian concept! I hope that one day we will realize the importance of autism knowledge and realize this aspect of autopia, but I also acknowledge that within the current state of education the following suggestions are unlikely to be fulfilled easily.

Qualifications

I genuinely feel that key contact staff – in other words those with direct contact with a child for the majority of the child's time in school – should have an autism qualification that is endorsed by the autistic community. By qualification I mean a course that is run by an accredited body for which the individual needs to apply, attend, and submit work to demonstrate that they have met the requirements. In addition to those staff, the whole leadership team and SENDCo (special educational needs and/or disabilities coordinator) should have the same qualification.

The above applies to mainstream schools. Within a special school, a resource, and autism specialist school the argument would be for all eligible staff to have a post-graduate autism qualification. For those who are unable to access post-graduate level an alternative academic qualification at the appropriate level should be provided.

Who should be trained and who should train?

As well as the above qualifications, all staff within school should have a clear individual CPD autism-specific programme that is a mandatory requirement covering all aspects of autism, teaching and learning. In terms of who should provide the training, it should wherever possible be autistic-led.

Inclusion

How to be inclusive – what does inclusion even mean?

Inclusion must be based on autistic quality of life. *Inclusion is not synonymous with integration, and equality is not the same as equity.* These are essential concepts to agree upon. Integration is the notion that children should share the same spaces together, whereas inclusion should be based on providing an education in which all children feel valued and educated taking their individual needs into account. Equality suggests that children should be provided with the same resources, whereas equity provides the necessary resources for a successful outcome for each child.

Autopia absolutely embraces the concept that to be fully inclusive, any environment must ensure that the child:

- feels safe
- is happy
- is understood
- is accepted
- feels included
- has their individual needs met.

Please note, the 'feels included' is not the same (necessarily) as integration. For example, your child might feel fully included if she is given a role that differs from most of the other children. Feeling included might also mean that the school has embraced diversity to the point of a huge change in culture. Culture change cannot be underestimated in terms of how powerful it might be. Imagine a culture in which it is perfectly usual for the head teacher to wear a onesie, where fidget spinners are habitually available as part of the lesson plans, where children share their stories around difference, where ND teachers are visible, where ear defenders are the norm not the exception – the list could go on. None of these is an extraordinary example of inclusive practice (well, head teachers might disagree on the onesie I guess), but collectively they denote a culture in which your child is more likely to feel 'at home'. True inclusion is about this culture of acceptance of difference and embracing the richness that comes with it.

World Book Day, Children in Need, school trips

The days that are not traditional school days, such as those in the above heading, are not invariably autism friendly. It is absolutely the school's responsibility to identify how to ensure that all children feel they are included at such times taking the above list into account. 'Simply' giving the child the option of not attending on that day is not the answer! It *might* be a solution for some children, but if it is the *only* option provided then the school is not doing enough.

Anomaly days such as World Book Day could cause anxiety for some (and might be absolutely loved by others), so ensure that the child does not stand out. Accept that some children will find such change in routine unsettling and make sure that there is an ethos in the school of no one size fits all. Make sure that some teachers come to school in their usual clothes, and that it is clear throughout school that not 'conforming' to convention is a healthy and absolutely acceptable option to all.

School play

All children can be included in the school play – given enough imagination. From working on the programme of events, to designing costumes, to being in charge of the spotlight, to being a prompter, to writing scripts, to being the lead acting role – there is a role for every child, and all children need to feel just as included as anyone else.

Masking

I was interested to read today about a rugby player and how she feels that her portrayal as a person is sometimes judged by her aggressive play on the pitch. It got me thinking about masking, and how so many autistic children mask – and what masking even means. Despite the rugby player's 'persona' on the pitch being extremely different from the passive, caring individual she is when she is off it, she is not masking when she is playing the sport – it is simply a different facet of her personality. So many people, when learning about autistic masking, make the mistake of thinking 'well, we all mask a lot of the time'. I am not at all sure that this is the case; I feel that many people will have different aspects of their personalities that they utilize in different situations, most of which take little or no effort. As a teacher, teaching in front of a class is not the same as how you will behave (presumably, anyway) when you are at home with your partner. Does that mean that you are masking at school (or, even, at home)? I don't think so – my belief is that you are behaving in a different way to suit that particular occasion, and that it doesn't take a particularly huge effort to do so; in fact, I suspect that very few people have to make the huge effort that so many autistic people identify when it comes to genuine masking.

Autistic masking stems from pressure to conform in many cases. Being 'naturally autistic' is often frowned upon, and from a very early age many children are 'encouraged' to behave in ways that are unnatural to them. This is a crucial point; *autistic masking is not a natural component of everyday life* – it takes considerable effort to do, and takes considerable energy to do it. For many of the PNT, behaving in slightly different ways in different social situations is still a natural part of their behavioural compass. This isn't to dismiss the very real anxiety that some people will suffer from in certain situations in which they have to concentrate hard to get through it effectively; as an arbitrary example, a best man might get very anxious when giving his speech. He may be making a huge effort to 'get it right' and the anxiety might well stem from the pressure he is under and the big occasion – but he is still himself. Autistic masking is very different – it is forcing one's self to act in an unnatural way that is at the very least uncomfortable, and at worst causes trauma over a period of time.

Continuing with the sports parallels, while watching the snooker World Championships I was struck by a player with a very unusual cue action, in particular his 'bridge' for the cue. As an autism obsessive, I tend to link almost everything in my life to autism; in this case I reflected on the fact that it was this marked difference that presumably contributed in some way towards him being a world-class player. I then wondered whether he would have been such a world-class player if, when he started playing, he'd been encouraged (or forced) to adopt a more standard approach. Now, I don't know what the answer is – maybe he would still have ended up on the world stage, who knows – but I do hypothesize that being forced into an unnatural way of playing would have taken more effort than being allowed to play in a way that suits his particular style, irrespective of how most other players play the game. I feel that this is similar to the autistic child who is encouraged (or forced) to behave in ways that are unnatural to her – again, it will take a much greater effort, quite possibly to achieve a sub-standard result. And yet, society encourages masking in so many ways, as opposed to accepting that for some children, their natural way of engaging might better suit not just them but broader society.

Masking has the additional problem of giving false impressions. An effective masker is not only making an effort to behave in ways that are unnatural, using up energy in the process (often to the extreme detriment to his learning ability), he is also giving a false impression to any observer. Often, at school, a child's masking will hide aspects such as anxiety – which is obviously a very real problem. If teaching staff are unaware of the depth of a child's anxiety as a direct result of masking, then it is unlikely that they will realize that a situation is causing stress; subsequently there is a triple whammy: the child is using up energy by masking and is learning less effectively; the child is in a high state of anxiety; and no one then believes him or his parent when they try to articulate how much school is causing stress.

It is not difficult to identify common practice that encourages masking; from a young age a child will often be told to suppress behaviour that is natural to them, even though that behaviour is communicating an emotional state. Take the very simplistic example of a young girl who squeaks whenever she is nervous. Society has deemed it a negative thing, so whenever she squeaks she is told to be quiet. She learns to mask – in this case having to quash her natural instinct to squeak – and thus loses her ability to communicate when she is nervous. This might sound like a trite example, but if you amplify this on a daily basis and consider how much natural autistic behaviour we attempt to modify it becomes so much easier to understand how much of the autistic life is spent trying to conform as a direct result of being encouraged to do so. Imagine, then, going back to the simplistic example, that squeaking becomes a perfectly acceptable communicative noise – much in the same way that shouting 'ow' is currently a perfectly acceptable communicative noise to communicate pain. If autistic expression is accepted and understood then there would be less chance of the need for masking, and a reduction of risk of trauma to the child (and, indeed, adult). As in so much of the book, it comes down to a genuine acceptance of being autistic, as opposed to trying to change being autistic to fit in more effectively with the PNT; the 'lesser' model again rears its ugly head.

The more that difference is encouraged as opposed to discouraged, accepted rather than rejected, and embraced as part and parcel of humanity, the greater the chances of children living high-quality lives. Masking can be a life-long ordeal. Masking is learned from an early age – if we changed our attitude then we could avoid the need for masking and promote healthy autistic lives.

Autopia would be a society in which masking is no longer required; in line with so many of the autopian values this largely comes down, quite simply (!), to understanding and acceptance. If we were to understand why a person is masking, and remove the necessity for them to do so, and accept autistic ways of engaging as part of the natural scheme of humankind, then there would be a much greater chance of children turning into happy adults. On this point, it is well worth noting that a childhood of masking can often lead to a lack of autism recognition. I know of so many adults who end up getting a late identification. Sometimes this is when their own child is identified, sometimes it is when life has taken a turn for the worse and they no longer have the energy required to mask. Whatever the reason, I do know of adults who have become consciously aware of just how debilitating masking can be, and so deliberately choose to reduce or eliminate their masking behaviour. This can have major implications for the adult – some positive, but some negative. I know of individuals, for example, who are accused of no longer being themselves, whose partners have left them, who have lost friends or relatives as a result of becoming their true selves. If masking was avoided from the outset then the risk of these negative repercussions would be reduced.

'School refusal'

Do children really refuse to go to school – or are they in such a state of distress that the only way that they can survive is to avoid what is causing that distress? The very term 'school refuser' in this context is abhorrent to me; it firmly points a finger of blame towards the child, and surreptitiously (or even overtly) suggests that the child is the one at fault. The message is clear – the child needs to change in some way to get back into school. If we completely changed the perception of the child, and created a new conceptual model whereby the automatic assumption was that school is somehow problematic as opposed to the child, then it would be much more likely that a suitable solution would be identified. Continuous expectations that the child is at fault are usually unhelpful at the very least. Please note that I have suggested that the automatic assumption is that there is a problem with the school – but that doesn't mean that it is always the case. However, addressing the current imbalance by reversing the trend is much more likely to be supportive of the child.

While on the note of the school refuser – or, let's refer to the child for whom school has let them down – autopia would no longer support the line of inquiry of 'how can we get the child back into school?'. Instead, autopia would pose the following questions:

- What has potentially caused the child such distress that they cannot access school?
- What can school do to make adjustments to reduce distress to the child?
- Has there been any irreversible trauma done to the child – in which case could the child going back to the same school increase their trauma?
- Is this model of school an appropriate one to suit this child at this time, or should we be seeking an alternative?
- What support is being provided to parents/family while the child is recovering at home?
- How can we reduce the risk of this happening again (for this child and for any other)?

6

Beyond school

Friendships

I have made some comments on friendships already, but it is perhaps worth reiterating as a section in its own right that many children will have friendships that don't necessarily align with what tends to be expected within the PNT. This is fine so long as your child is content. That is absolutely the most important aspect in relation to friendships – that the child is content. It is worth asking what a child actually needs in terms of a friendship, then matching it up with what the child currently has. For example, if a child yearns for companionship, within a relationship that doesn't judge, is there for her when she chooses, and you realize that she ticks all of those boxes with the family dog, then what is the problem? The notion that everyone *needs* friends is simply not accurate. Some children will need relationships to enable them to be fulfilled, but this is not always the case. Some children will want friends at some points in life but not others, some will prefer their relationships to be online (it goes without saying that safety issues here also need to be addressed) – there are endless possibilities that might suit your child that are less than traditional. I feel sometimes that children need permission not to have to fit in with everyone else's way of doing things.

In autopia there is no judgement around relationships; if a child wants to be best friends with a 66-year-old then this is perfectly acceptable. If a child's best friend is the collection of *Harry Potter* books then so be it. If a child chooses to invite folk to his birthday party and remain upstairs, then good for him.

Free time

Free time can be difficult for children when they don't know how best to fill it. It might be useful to reconsider free time and replace it with the concept of down time. Life for your child is very much about balance and energy; recognizing when energy batteries need recharging and – just as importantly – knowing how to recharge them is vital for their equilibrium. Listing things around energy can be a great way to support a child (or adult, come to think of it). Having lists of people who can be divided into energy takers and energy givers can be so useful in allowing your child a clearer perspective as to how, when, and where to engage with others. Similarly, having lists of activities that give or take energy can be so useful; when it comes to unstructured 'free time' the child can then ascertain what her energy levels are and how best to use the time – either to engage with others if that suits, or recharge her energy levels if that is what is required.

Making choices

So often we are told that children find making choices difficult. However, just as often I find that it is the lack of knowledge as to what is on offer that is the issue, not making the choice itself. This is where open-ended choices can be problematic – after all, logically an open-ended question can lead to unlimited answers, in which case how is anyone in a position to make a considered choice? It is far better working with a child around choice making and gradually building up the choices available, rather than expecting the child to develop the skill on her own. For children who cannot respond to open-ended choices, limiting choices is actually giving him far greater options. For example, limiting a choice down to three options gives the child three more options than the open-ended question! Subsequently increasing those options will develop his abilities to make considered choices in the future.

I tend to think that the sooner choice making is explicitly addressed, the better. If at a young age a child is able to explore choice making and decision making in a non-threatening environment, the better their chances are of him being able to make considered choices later on in life. It might be useful to start with to give a choice that you know will stimulate him; the offer of two activities, one of which you know is a preferred activity, can be a nice easy choice to make – and you can work your way forward from there. Within this choice-making process, though, it is wise to be clear that at times it is ok to choose something that is not offered as an option to ensure that the child remains safe.

Screen time

Some children will appear to be addicted to screens. Before you despair, though, ask yourself whether the perceived problem is actually a problem, or a more general feeling from society. Generations of people differ – adult generations grew up doing things differently to their children. The imposition of older generational expectations might also therefore need to change. I am constantly amused when thinking about my own generation who were constantly told to stop watching television compared to this generation who are sometimes asked to stop looking at their screens – to come and watch television with their parents!

Of course, excessive screen time may be a very real problem, but looking at a screen per se is not an issue. What the child is engaging with is obviously important, but say for example the child is engaging with a passionate interest then maybe he is having the best time of his life – and why shouldn't he?

Holidays

Holidays are often a rather 'love them or hate them' time for children. Some will love the escape from school and yearn for holiday time while others may find holidays daunting. For the latter group having some level of structure may well be necessary; I don't believe that it's the holidays per se that are the issue (i.e. the not going to school bit) – it tends to be the lack of routine, lack of clear expectation, and not knowing what is happening on a day-to-day basis that can be problematic. Then there are the actual going away holidays that might also cause stress – the fear of the unknown.

Interventions

Ok, so a book on what works for autistic children probably shouldn't avoid the very contentious issue of behavioural interventions. It's a very divisive subject indeed, with one side claiming that interventions are a necessary and positive part of life and the other side saying that they can be harmful, unethical, and with long-term negative consequences. The easiest option for autopia is to start with the extreme. The original applications of Applied Behaviour Analysis (ABA) in which children were physically harmed in order to change their behaviour were clearly abhorrent and cruel. Behavioural techniques have changed since then, but there are still elements of behaviour programmes that do not sit comfortably within autopia, for the following reasons (note – I refer to behaviour programmes in general rather than any specific behaviour technique here):

- Withholding or limiting access to what is precious to the child
- Who decides on what is the 'right' behaviour?
- Is the programme trying to get the child to behave more like the PNT – if so, why?
- Much of the language in behaviour programmes does not align to autopian language values
- Autism is not behaviour.

Withholding or limiting access to what is precious to the child

Some programmes encourage practitioners to withhold something of value to the child if the child is not 'compliant' – in other words, if the child does not do what is wanted then she does not get her reward, which is commonly something that is precious to her. Not allowing access to something that is precious to a child in order to change behaviour seems like a problematic concept to me. Children will always display a behaviour for a reason – it is not always clear what that reason is, but there will always be one. If a child, for example, is hitting someone sat next to him and the therapist decides that this is unwanted behaviour, then that behaviour could well be changed in some way using techniques such as withholding a reward when the behaviour occurs and giving the reward when it doesn't. This may well seem to work (i.e. the child eventually stops hitting). However, this doesn't make any attempt to understand why the behaviour is occurring in the first instance. If, for example, the child is hitting the person sat next to him because it seems like the best way to get her to move away which is a necessity, as she is causing him distress (e.g. for a sensory reason), then the outcome of the behavioural technique for the child is that the problem remains, but he is no longer able to deal with it. So, not only has the child had to endure a punishment/reward system (and autistic adults tell us that this can cause trauma) but he has learned that he must put up with his distress. If, on the other hand, the problem is identified as stemming from a sensory issue, first and foremost the environment needs to change in order to take away the distress, while in the longer term the child can be supported in their communication skills around how to demonstrate when they are in distress.

Who decides on what is the 'right' behaviour?

This is one of the fundamental issues that autopia has with many behavioural programmes. Who decides on what is deemed 'good' behaviour? The worrying aspect for me is the number of children who are encouraged (or forced) to change what is inoffensive autistic behaviour simply because it is not the norm, and changed to become more compliant with those around them. Autopia is a culture in which difference is seen as celebratory, not a negative. Some might argue that displaying behaviour that stands out from the norm will leave children vulnerable to teasing, bullying, and discrimination. I agree. What I don't agree with – emphatically disagree with, in fact – is the notion that the problem then lies within the child. The problem is with those who tease, bully and discriminate.

There may be all sorts of unwanted behaviours associated with your child. These should not be labelled as challenging, and nor should they ever only be understood at a behavioural level. Most children displaying behaviours that others deem as challenging are doing so from a distressed state. Removing the distress will be far more effective at supporting the child than solely changing the behaviour.

Is the programme trying to get the child to behave more like the PNT – if so, why?

In a similar vein as the above, some programmes seem to assume that the PNT way of behaving in any given environment is a norm to aspire to. This 'everyone else does it that way' approach can be very dangerous to the child. In some circumstances I see this approach akin to the old-style rejection of children being left-handed; being struck on the left hand every time a child uses it simply because most children are right-handed is clearly immoral. I have certainly come across situations in which children are similarly treated when displaying perfectly harmless natural autistic behaviour. Autopia is an existence in which behaving differently (not badly) to others is never automatically deemed problematic. In my book on anxiety these are the questions I suggest around behaviour, and they are worth repeating here:

- Are we trying to change behaviour for the sake of the child – is it really what's best for the child?
- Do we understand why the child is behaving in this way currently? If not, do we understand the risks of changing that behaviour?
- Are we trying to make the child adapt behaviour just because that is how most other kids behave?
- Is the behaviour a naturally and harmless autistic way of being? If so, why are we trying to change it?
- What are the intended outcomes if we are trying to change the behaviour?
- Are we sure that this is not going to cause undue anxiety for the child?
- Are we aware of the potential longer-term implications of changing behaviour?
- Have we considered that the behaviour might well change over time without intervention?
- How problematic is the behaviour anyway?

For a more detailed narrative around these questions see if your local library has the anxiety book and take a read!

Much of the language in behaviour programmes does not align to autopian language values

As noted earlier in the section on language, autopia rejects the almost constant litany of negative pejorative language that litters the autism narrative. Very often, behaviour programmes are the source of many such language issues – aberrant behaviour that is unwanted, challenging, violent or aggressive – these are all terms that can frequently be found in behaviour programmes, which seem to me to increase the risk of the finger pointing of blame towards the child, rather than the situation that the child finds herself in.

Autism is not behaviour

As I have written in other books, autism is not behaviour. If you come across any programme that claims in any way that by changing the behaviour of your child equates to making your child less autistic or even not autistic, then run away immediately.

The happy autopian child

Last of all – and I recognize that this book could have been three times longer to cover way more issues than I have been able to – I would like to provide some options for what I believe will lead to the happy autopian child.

- Allowed to identify as autistic
- Understands what it means to be autistic
- Can develop at their own pace rather than having to meet PNT milestones
- Age appropriateness doesn't exist
- Language is life-affirming not negative
- Autistic authenticity
- Access to animals
- The child is at the centre of decision making
- Being naturally autistic is accepted, embraced, encouraged.

Allowed to identify as autistic

The sooner your child knows she is autistic the better in my view. If your child is left unidentified then she will very likely start to get an understanding of autism that is not likely to be beneficial. As has been pointed out, much of the current language and notions of autism are inherently negative, so if your child learns to think about autism (however subconsciously) in a negative perspective then when she is identified as autistic it may already be problematic for her.

However, if we have a culture of identification at as young an age as possible then your child can grow up knowing who she is from the outset. I've written elsewhere about suggested ways of allowing your child to understand herself; needless to say, within autopia she will be able to learn from parents and those around her what it means to be autistic, what it means to be her, how to understand self and how to best make use of the exquisite knowledge to give her the best chances in life.

Understand what it means to be autistic

Understanding what it means to be autistic, as alluded to above, is to provide a child with the opportunities to genuinely have an understanding of self. Without the knowledge as to who he is, what an intrinsic component of his very being means, is to gravely risk a misjudged self and potential damage to self-esteem and wellbeing. The opposite is also the case – having that knowledge can make all the difference between judging one's self against an impossible set of criteria (i.e. the PNT) and losing at every stage, or allowing one's self to understand life through one's own autism lens are recognizing that one is, in fact, not a sub-standard PNT but a perfectly well-adjusted autistic.

Can develop at their own pace rather than having to meet PNT milestones

With everyone knowing that your child is autistic within autopia means that the judgements and decisions about how, what and when to develop within a PNT context can be safely ignored. Instead, your child will be allowed to develop at her own pace, within her own parameters, aligned with her own motivation without judgement. So many children so much of the time end up with self-esteem issues because of their spiky profile, because they are deemed 'behind' others of a similar age; in reality, they are simply developing different skills in different ways. In many cases the skills deemed a necessity at age five will develop naturally so that within a couple of years there is no problem anyway. The problem arises from the pressure on the child and the parent to develop in a way that is unnatural and, often, incredibly challenging at that time. Being given the time to develop naturally without that judgement takes all the pressure off.

Age appropriateness doesn't exist

I am not at all convinced that age appropriateness (outside of an abusive context, of course) is anything that has a place within autopia. Adults are encouraged to behave in childish ways should they choose to do so, children can behave in an adult manner if that is their way of being. People are people – children are not rubbish adults, and adults are not rubbish children. Why society seems to place boundaries around behaviour and lifestyle dependent on age is beyond me. I am very happy to declare that recently I have re-read all of the *Pippi Longstocking* books from my childhood and received one of my best birthday presents ever in the form of a toy Moomin who comes to bed with me every night.

Language is life-affirming not negative

I think you will have got the message loud and clear by now, but autopia's language around autism is consistently life-affirming, celebrating humankind without making any assumptions that any neurotype is better or worse than any other.

Autistic authenticity

The very concept of autistic authenticity is both a joy and a problem. It is joyful in that allowing a child to be their authentic self is something wonderful, and celebrating autistic authenticity is something we should all engage in. However, the very notion that we need to point this out just demonstrates how far we have to go; all children should be allowed to be authentic as a given – not as a goal.

Access to animals

Never underestimate the power of the impact of animals on the child. Having a friendly animal (of whatever variety suited to the child) can be an absolute game changer. Having a non-judgemental furry or feathery friend (other options also available) who is reliable and trustworthy cannot be underestimated in the level of joy it can bring. Add to this the sensory heaven of said beast and we can start to understand the importance of an autopian menagerie.

The child is at the centre of decision making

Finding your child's 'voice' (in whatever way that might be) is critical. It might be through mediums other than speech, it could be photography, dance, video gaming – the list is endless. However you find her voice, autopia is keen that subsequently all decisions around her engagement are based on her wellbeing and long-term success. No longer should children be driven by what society thinks is best for them – decisions must take her voice into account and support her to go against the societal tide if that is what, ultimately, is best for her autistic self.

Being naturally autistic is accepted, embraced, encouraged

It is long overdue that autistic children are recognized as an integral population within society, and they are no longer treated and understood as lesser. If wider society genuinely had a better understanding, if people were more accepting, more knowledgeable, less afraid of difference – none of which costs anything – autistic lives would benefit. Autopia, at least some aspects of it, will happen. And it will change lives in a positive way, for ever.

A few years ago I was involved in collating chapters for a book called *Bittersweet on the Autism Spectrum* and was in contact with a woman from Australia called Alyssa. I was allowed to read her chapter and provide a short introduction to it, and I very often finish talks with her words, as the quotation is, I think, one of the most beautiful pieces of narrative in the autism arena that I have ever read. I have slightly updated the quotation but the sentiment is exactly the same. I have written this book as a conduit; it is the shared autistic experiences that have meant I have been able to write it, so it is only fitting that I conclude with someone else's words:

'The privilege of being oneself is a gift many take for granted, but for an autistic person, being allowed to be oneself is the greatest and rarest gift of all' (Alyssa Aleksanian, 2016).

Index